Be Merry

How To Advent
Without Losing Your Mind

By Sterling Jaquith

Published by Ever Catholic
Boise, ID 83704

Copyeditor: Cayla Mello
Cover Design: Sterling Jaquith

ISBN: 978-1-946076-03-8

Dedication

I dedicate this book to my loving parents
Shannon Peake and Marylou Bryant.

Yes, you did work a lot during the holidays, but I always felt loved. You sacrificed so much to give me space to learn and grow. I would not be the writer or the faithful woman that I am without you both!

Table of Contents

Introduction

Saints before the altar bending,
Watching long in hope and fear,
Suddenly the Lord, descending,
In His temple shall appear:
Come and worship,
Come and worship,
Worship Christ, the newborn King!

- *Angels from the Realms of Glory By James Montgomery*[i]

The holidays are a time of bright colors, twinkling lights, and cheery music. There are parties, decorations, gifts, delicious food, and fun activities happening nearly every day. But for many of us, November 1st through January 2nd represents nothing but anxiety, stress, and often depression. We dread the upcoming battles we'll have to fight even if we're just battling our own expectations.

We may each suffer from very different struggles during the holiday season. Accordingly, we will need to employ different strategies to maintain positive attitudes and peace during a time that can so easily be co-opted by the world. That is what this book contains: strategies.

This book will offer you peace. It will give you real practical tips that you can apply to your life to create a more harmonious holiday season for yourself.

I will cover practical tips for dealing with your marriage, your extended family, and any misguided attempts at decorating and gift giving that you might have. I'll also help you learn how to avoid anxiety and depression, or deal with anxiety and depression should they show up. Most importantly, I'll invite you to find genuine joy in celebrating our beautiful Catholic faith this holiday season.

It really is possible to have joy and to stay connected to Jesus despite the noise and distractions the world will throw at you.

I grew up with divorced parents who both worked in the jewelry industry. This occupation means that, because of the intensity of holiday sales, they were the most overworked and stressed during what should be the most joyful time of year. I grew up dreading November and December. I longed for winter break to be over so I could go back to school. Yet, I was also embarrassed to begin the "what did you get for Christmas" conversations – knowing that I had a poor showing.

Even after becoming Christian, I still retained a dark view of the holidays. I've had to work hard over the last many years to realize that through Christ I have both the knowledge and the grace to participate in the real meaning of Christmas. I can overcome past hurts and choose to love the people who are in my life right now. I have the capacity for great mercy and forgiveness in sticky family situations.

I have learned to temper my expectations about decorating and gift giving so that I'm focusing on what the holidays should be about – creating an atmosphere of peace, serving others out of love, and celebrating that Jesus came into the world.

I can increase my prayer time and spend more time reading the word of God so that I remember why we're celebrating Christmas in the first place. I can prioritize Advent traditions to help my children experience the beautiful rhythms of the Catholic Church.

Last, I can acknowledge that the holidays are often a time I feel anxious and become depressed. By staying ahead of these emotions and being prepared to deal with them as soon as they bubble up, I can avoid the deep and dark negative spiral that steals my joy during the holidays.

It is my hope that you too would have a solid plan in place for managing the many challenges that arise during the holidays, allowing you to float through these months with peace and contentment. Yes, even if you have a calendar that is booked like crazy!

Heading into this year's holiday festivities, I want you to feel empowered to deal with the challenges that may be brought on by your friends, your family, and your own emotions. This power can only come by first naming the problem and then creating an action plan that starts with clinging tightly to Jesus.

The holidays should be a time of great joy, but it takes effort. To realize this joy that the holiday season can offer, we may need to retrain our minds and strengthen our resolve.

Join me as we choose to Be Merry this year because Jesus really is the reason for the season!

Marriage

Veil'd in Flesh the Godhead see,
Hail th' incarnate Deity!
Pleas'd as Man with Men t'appear,
Jesus our Emmanuel here.

- Hark! The Herald Angels Sing by Charles Wesley[ii]

Christmas is not about a birth; it's about a marriage – a marriage of divinity to humanity. Two becoming one flesh, the divine person of Jesus with the human person of Jesus.

I want to start with marriage because it is the foundation from which we make so many of our decisions. Our first memories of Christmas are framed within marriage. This is true whether we had married or divorced parents. Whatever relationship our parents had when we were growing up largely shapes our view of the holidays as an adult.

Later in this book, we will talk about past holidays, especially the ones we experienced growing up. We will examine those memories and truly ask ourselves how they affect our experience of holidays now. But first, I want to talk about your own marriage.

Once we are married ourselves, we blend two different sets of ideas and traditions about the holidays. Because we are tied together with our spouse, for better or worse, as one flesh, we cannot have vastly different experiences of the holidays. If one of you is rather sulky, the other will have their joy dampened. If one of you is filled with anxiety, it will be hard for the other to sit peacefully in front of the white lights of your Christmas tree.

Marriage is the biggest factor that determines whether our holiday season will be smooth sailing or filled with rocky waters. Whether we are actively engaged as a team with our spouse, or we are simply desperate to avoid confrontation, the current state of our marriage makes a big difference.

It can be difficult to find genuine joy during the holidays when we have different expectations and plans from our spouse for the frenzied months of November and December. My first Christmas with my husband is a great example of this.

Our First Christmas

What Child is this
Who laid to rest
On Mary's lap is sleeping?
Whom Angels greet with anthems sweet,
While shepherds watch are keeping?

- *What Child Is This? By William Chatterton Dixiii*

To say that my husband and I were unprepared for our first holiday season would be a huge understatement. Wide-eyed and in love, I thought our first Christmas was going to be magical. I thought it was going to be sprinkled with kisses, laughing, delicious food, the perfect presents, and the start of our own family traditions.

That year was going to be my Hallmark Christmas!

I'm not sure why I was so confident about how we would experience the holidays. Up until Christmas morning, we had never talked about what our expectations were. I just assumed we would want the same things.

You must understand that my husband and I didn't have a great marriage prep experience. In fact, the priest in charge of our marriage prep was one foot out the door on his way to a new parish assignment. We had one meeting where we took a scantron test. He told us to discuss the answers that were different, handed us a book about NFP, and sent us on our way. That was the extent of what we received for "marriage prep."

The topic of holidays remained unspoken until we got to that very first Christmas. I remember that day clearly. We had enjoyed a lovely and quiet breakfast together and a slow afternoon. It was almost time to leave to head to my grandmother's house for Christmas dinner. My husband came out of the bedroom wearing jeans and a t-shirt.

I said, "You need to get ready. We have to leave soon."

He said, "I am ready.

I responded, "Oh… well…you can't wear *that.* You need to be dressed up. I mean we're going to Christmas Dinner!"

Looking confused, he replied, "Oh, I thought it was only your family. I thought we were just going over to relax at your grandmother's house."

Sounding annoyed, and feeling a bit embarrassed, I said, "Yeah, I mean it is just my family, but you at least need to be wearing slacks and a sweater. It's Christmas." I just kept repeating "it's Christmas," as if somehow it would sink in that this was a formal holiday and he would suddenly understand the need for formal clothes.

My first mistake was assuming that everyone has formal holiday gatherings with their family.

My husband does not like wearing uncomfortable clothes. He will go great lengths to avoid wearing anything stiff or tight. While I had learned this about him in our few months of being married, I never imagined that Christmas would be included in the list of things he wouldn't dress up for.

I remember thinking, "It's not a big deal. Can't you just throw on a sweater? Can't you just do this for me?"

To my great disappointment, he didn't suddenly come to understand the need for fancy clothes and so began the first of our holiday squabbles.

Our first Christmas devolved from there. We had many more misunderstandings, disagreements, and philosophical differences about how to celebrate this joyful holiday. I'd love to say that we smoothed everything out that year, but we didn't. We had to suffer a few more rocky holidays before discovering some strategies for managing our expectations and creating routines.

Before I discuss these tips, I want to discuss how important marriage prep really is for anyone who hasn't gotten married or who knows someone about to get married.

I know that many couples are blessed with a wonderful and deep marriage prep experience. Even good programs may not cover the importance of holiday planning, though. If you are newly married and heading into your first holiday season, but have not yet discussed holiday expectations with your spouse, now is a great time to have this discussion. If you know someone who is engaged or newly married, you might mention to them that planning the holidays before they come up is a great way to make sure you're still married in January!

What are you going to do on Thanksgiving?

Whose house will you go to for Christmas?

What's your gift giving and receiving plan?

Are you going to dress casually or formally for these events?

Describe your expectations to each other for what will happen on Christmas Day.

Since my husband and I didn't make time to discuss these questions, we experienced a huge clash of expectations. This happened to us many times before we were finally able to agree about how our family would celebrate the holidays. Save yourself some heartache and have the holidays conversation as soon as possible!

The Turning Point

For He is our childhood's pattern;
Day by day, like us, He grew;
He was little, weak, and helpless,
Tears and smiles, like us He knew;
And He cares when we are sad,
And he shares when we are glad.

- *Once In Royal David's City*

A few years into our marriage, we were once again driving to my grandmother's for Christmas Dinner. I was sitting in the passenger seat staring out the window at the cheery, colorful lights passing by. I felt anything but cheerful, though. We were both seethingly mad, and you could feel the tension in the car. It was dark outside, and our moods were as cold as the frozen lawns we were passing.

We had been squabbling all day about a bunch of silly little things. We both knew that if either of us said anything, we would explode into a big argument. My husband and I try very hard not to argue in front of kids, so the only alternative was to sit in absolute silence.

I remember thinking, "How could he ruin my Christmas? Why couldn't he just do what I wanted for this one simple day?"

To know how we arrived at this situation, this moment of being so mad at each other on a day that's supposed to be filled with joy, I think you need to understand a little bit about how we grew up.

My husband comes from a much bigger family than I do and they had large Christmas gatherings. They would all hole up in a house in Northern Michigan for a few days like a big cozy sleepover of grandparents, aunts, and cousins.

They would play in the snow, drink hot chocolate, trounce each other in board games, and spend real quality time with each other. The adults would all help cook Christmas dinner, and everyone would come together to clean up. It's clear that they did exchange some presents, but this wasn't a big part of their Christmas day. He has fond memories of the holidays and this special time he got to relax with his extended family.

I had a very different Christmas experience. My mother (who was a single mom) worked in retail – which means that I barely saw her for most of the Christmas season. On Christmas morning, we would wake up and open a few small presents. Christmas morning seemed to emphasize that we didn't have much money or a big family to celebrate with.

When I was in my teens, I would find out that my mom would wait to receive a few presents from her own mother, only to return them and then use that money to buy a few things for my brother and me. I'll talk more about my broken view of presents later on in the book.

Next, we would get dressed up, and my dad would take us to my grandmother's for Christmas Dinner. Her house was like a beautiful, glittering palace. She was a very formal lady, and her house was filled with porcelain dolls and glass figurines – hardly a place for children. Her dinner table was always sparkling with decorations. She had a special set of Christmas china, each plate set upon a gold charger. There were red crystal wine glasses and so much silverware that you didn't know what to do with it all.

We didn't go to church or Mass for Christmas, but we still dressed up in our nicest clothes. We were told to be quiet, stay out of the way, and not to break anything. We often played a board game, just my brother and I, until dinner. We were then relegated to a kid's table, largely left out of any conversation with the adults even though there were few present.

My grandmother was a Special Education teacher for over thirty years, and although she was always described to me as having the biggest and kindest heart, I'm not sure I ever met that version of her. We didn't have a close relationship. Although she did give us some presents, they were often things we were completely uninterested in which highlighted how little she knew about my brother and me.

I do believe that gratitude for gifts is important, but I think we all know when a gift is given out of obligation rather than love. In the end, Christmas was something I had to get through, rather than a holiday that I looked forward to.

My husband greatly missed the casual, warm, holidays of his childhood and I didn't understand why he couldn't just buck up and get through Christmas at my grandmother's as I had done for so many years.

Silence filled the car as we were driving that evening. We stared out our windows ignoring each other and our hurt feelings. I imagine we were both mourning the idea of the perfect Christmas that we had hope for upon waking up that morning.

It wasn't just the issue of dressing fancy vs. dressing casually that divided us. We'd had disagreements over presents to buy, food that we should bring, how long we would stay, and how to react when receiving gifts. My family thought that fake reactions of happiness upon receiving a gift were a nice way to make someone feel appreciated. My husband thought this was akin to lying.

It had been a series of arguments throughout the day that led up to this stalemate in the car. I remember feeling so bitter, thinking, "Why is he ruining this for me? It's just a sweater. Is it such a big deal to just do what I want?"

In that dark and frozen moment, riding in the car, I felt like someone put their hand on my shoulder and asked, "What about him?

I don't know who whispered that in my ear. I don't know if it was Jesus, Mary, my guardian angel, or one of the many fabulous saints who look out for me, but I heard that question loud and clear.

"What about him?"

At first, I thought this question was about Jesus. *You know Sterling, you're sounding pretty self-centered right now. You're being really selfish. Where is Jesus in all this? How are you bringing Jesus to your kids right now...to your extended family?*

Jesus hadn't been part of any conversation we had that day. On His very birthday, we had left Him in the background.

The second thought I had was, "What about him? What about my husband?"

What about this man who had sacrificed so much for me? Here I was whining like a teenager about not getting my way. I hadn't asked myself even once what I could do to make his Christmas special. My poor husband doesn't even get to see his family on Christmas because they're thousands of miles away and I hadn't done anything special to make him feel loved.

We adore his family. We miss them and wish desperately that we could see them on Christmas. Up until this moment, I wasn't even thinking about them. I hadn't considered that he might be sad. I wasn't caring for his heart.

I was doing a pretty terrible job of being his wife.

As we pulled into my grandmother's driveway, I put my hand on his hand, and I did something that was very hard. I said, "You know what honey, I'm sorry. I wasn't being very nice to you today. I shouldn't have spoken to you like that. I'm sorry for trying to impress my family instead of choosing you."

In some moments, God makes our priorities very clear. We are supposed to love God the most, then our spouse, then our children, and then everyone else. I had gotten this backward all day.

It's easy to make this mistake because the "everyone else" group tends to be the loudest and most urgent voice. If your mother-in-law is a control freak who tries to make you feel guilty for not living up to her standards, it's difficult not to respond. We scramble to alleviate that pain – or act aggressively to prevent it from happening.

We feel safe being snarky with our husband or yelling at our children because we know they'll be there tomorrow. They can't get away, and we tell ourselves that they'll still love us. We risk the discomfort of our nuclear family to avoid certain pain from our extended family.

Some of us may only go one step higher on the life priority list and focus on making the holidays magical and memorable for our children. There is nothing wrong with this if we keep it all in balance. If however, our children become a higher priority than either our husband or our faith, then we are living in a disordered way.

I think there's a real opportunity for Catholic women to focus on those two people this year: Jesus and your husband.

I apologized to my husband, and I said, "I love you. I'm going to back you up in there tonight. I'm going to be on your team. I'm not going to throw you any squinty-faced looks across the room about something that you're doing. I'm not going to let them back you into a corner and make you feel uncomfortable. I'm going to be with you tonight."

I don't really remember what happened that particular Christmas, but I do know that every holiday since then my husband and I have gotten together to make a plan. We have a real conversation about our expectations for any major event whether it be Christmas, Easter, a baptism, or even just a big barbecue.

On the following pages are two exercises you can do with your spouse to help make sure you're on the same page this year. My husband and I have actually come to enjoy our "gearing up for the holiday" conversations instead of assuming they will be filled with tension. I think that's pretty miraculous in it of itself!

Read on to find out how you can team up with your spouse for the holidays!

Be A Team Exercise

As Catholic couples, it's so important that we get together and have these conversations. There's a real attack on Catholic and Christian families right now. The devil hates the family unit because when families love each other, they reflect the love of God into the world.

The devil is delighted when husbands and wives are in separate corners, pouting, and feeling unloved. His very name "Diablo" means "divider." He wants you to think, "My husband doesn't love me! He doesn't understand me!"

That's how the devil knows when he's winning. If he can divide a husband and a wife, he knows it can quickly lead to breaking up the family unit, and that there will be less of God's love in the world.

I want us to fight for the family. I want us to fight for Christian love. I want you to come together with your spouse and do this exercise.

1. Schedule a time when you can sit down with your spouse before the hustle and bustle of the holiday season. Tell your spouse it won't take long. Set a timer if you need to keep yourself accountable to a quick meeting.

2. When you're ready to start your meeting, begin the conversation by affirming your marriage.

   Honey, I love you. I'm so happy to be married to you. I'm grateful that you're my husband and I want to be on your team this year. Let's come up with a game plan for how we're going to tackle the holidays. Let me know what you want to be different this year.

   Watch as your spouse's mouth drops open with surprise that you're doing this.

3. Now shut up! No matter how badly you want to get more words in, your job is just to sit there and listen to what your spouse has to say. Don't object, don't clarify. If you need something physical to do to keep you from opening your mouth, then take notes. Just listen.

4. After your spouse is done talking, it's your turn. Pick a few specific things that you wish would be different this holiday season.

5. Last, make a game plan for how you will both work together this year to ensure a more pleasant holiday season.

"Operation Code Word" Exercise

One effective way you can be a team when attending big events is to have a code word. This is also a great tool that you can use when you see your spouse parenting your children in a way that you disagree with. Instead of arguing in front of the children, you say a code word like "hallway."

This means, "Whoa, I don't like what you're doing," or maybe "You don't have all the information, let me tell you something." In an effort to stand united in front of the children (and later in front of others at holiday events), we try to have these conversations in the hallway. When someone uses the code word, we step into the hallway (or another room) and have a quick chat about what's going on.

This is a really great strategy that you can apply to the holidays whether you're at a party or a dinner. You both agree on a code word that you each will remember. This code word can mean all sorts of things like, "Something's happening that's not great and I would love to talk to you for a minute."

But even if you use the code word for many different issues, it always means, let's step away from the hearing space of others to have a private conversation.

Maybe your husband's getting a little too political with your siblings. You see it getting heated and you want to calm that situation down. Maybe your husband sees you talking with your friends, he needs your help in the kitchen, and he just wants to bring your attention to that issue.

All of us have been witness to couples who argue in front of others. It's awkward and uncomfortable. It's worse when they enlist the opinions of bystanders in an attempt to "win." This public humiliation cuts more deeply than most of us would like to admit and stays with us far longer than the span of the event. Those wounds create insecurities in our marriages, and we carry them with us into future arguments.

By having a code word instead of an open argument, you and your spouse have an opportunity to affirm that you love each other and are on the same team. You're committed to supporting each other, and you will not add public humiliation to whatever sensitive issue you need to discuss.

Hopefully, this tool can take some of the edge off of your anxiety. You will likely feel calmer going into events – both because you have an option to resolve conflict and because you feel supported.

Most of us have experienced just how painful it is when our spouse undercuts us in public. When your husband makes a snarky comment or tells a joke that's a little cruel, it can hurt deeply. When we belittle our spouse, even in a lighthearted way, it can cause tension and pain in our marriage. It undermines the strength of our relationship. We are called to show God's love to the world through our marriage, yet so often we set such a bad example.

I'm not advocating that we have fake, plastic smiles and project a picture-perfect marriage to the world. Of course, marriage isn't good and fun all the time, but we should never put each other down publicly. Words of correction spoken publically not only cut more deeply but are more likely to be interpreted as an attack. Most disagreements can be handled in private.

Of course, it's also not appropriate to ridicule or attack your spouse privately, we must be gentle even when alone, but I'm sure there are whole marriage books on that topic!

We must be kind to our spouse. It is especially damaging to the public view of Catholicism to behave like cliquey teenagers who use insults to gain approval.

Be united as a team with your husband by using code words.

When Things Are Rocky

Lord, I will give my love to Thee,
Than gold much costlier.
Sweeter to Thee than frankincense,
More prized than the choicest myrrh,
Lord, make me dearer day by day,
Day by day holier; (Day by day holier).

- A Christmas Carol[iv]

I know some of you may be thinking, "Sterling, I don't know what you're talking about. I'm really struggling in my marriage right now. My husband is not going to sit down and talk with me to plan the holidays. There's no way he'll go for this code word idea."

I hear you. I have lived through awful patches in my marriage. I have touched the darkness and wondered if we were going to make it. Despite how bad it feels, I believe married couples can hit the reset button at any moment. Just like that Christmas in the car, I knew I had to do something radical to get us out of our gridlock. I had to apologize, ask for forgiveness, and commit to choosing my husband over my loud and judgmental family members.

I've often been the first one to extend the olive branch even when I didn't think that my husband deserved any type of forgiveness. I've even been rejected in these times, which hurts even more deeply than the original hurt. Sometimes it's my husband who has to initiate the make-up. We are called to do this over and over again. It is why marriage is a crucible that can reforge us until we are ready for Heaven.

Sometimes we simply have to humble ourselves to get our husbands to come back to the table. Affirm your marriage. He loves you too. He wants your marriage to be better too. If the civil conversation has failed, then your job is to pray.

There is power in a woman who prays. Pray for your husband and pray for your marriage. I would also suggest taking a real honest look at what you're doing to disrupt the harmony of your marriage. It's easy to think that the problem is just with our spouse.

"If only he would....we could be okay again." But that is not how marriage works. We are usually 50% of every problem we have. Until you can step back and recognize your contribution to the problem, it will be hard to make progress in your marriage. Start by acknowledging the petty, negative, hurtful things you're doing.

Tell him you're sorry with no expectation.

Ask for forgiveness and then give him space.

Educate yourself about your husband. What is his love language? What is his temperament type? What's his Myers-Briggs type?[v] Try to find out how God has created your unique husband, then love him through his uniqueness.

My husband and I have extremely different personalities. We have little in common besides our faith and parenting values. Our love languages are completely opposite. To help overcome this, we have read many books to help us understand each other, and we have learned so much!

I wish it hadn't taken us so many years to learn how to better handle each other. It's as if we each have our own language and need a few translators to bridge the gap and see that we are both trying. We do really love each other even if we keep misfiring our signals.

I also really enjoyed reading *Head and Heart* by Katie Warner[vi]. As someone who didn't grow up in a churched family, I really had no idea what a husband and wife's role should be, especially regarding faith. She describes how a man should be the spiritual leader of the family and woman should be the heart leader of her family. This helped me to let go of some things I was trying to control and to step up and manage some things I had been letting slide. This book is fantastic because she has clear action items at the end of each chapter that you can follow.

Katie talks about the importance of being the peace center of the household, and I realized that I was anything but peaceful during the holiday season. I had allowed the stress of organizing events, decorating the house, gift giving, and hosting guests to steal my joy. The more anxious I became, the less peace there was to be found in my home.

If you think you don't have time to read this great book, I will encourage you to do one of two things:

1. **Listen to an audio book version.** There are lots of free audiobooks on YouTube that you can listen to while you're cleaning or while you're in the car. You can get audiobooks at the library too!

2. **Read a summary.** If you don't have time for an audio book, search for the title of the book you're interested in and tack on the word "summary" at the end. Many people create detailed summaries of books that effectively convey the book content in far less time.

It's important always to be learning and growing. Reading (or listening to) books is one of the best ways we can continue our education. Be honest with yourself. You probably have twenty minutes a day to read a book that can help strengthen your marriage.

This year, I want you to put your marriage before all your other earthly relationships: those with your friends and even with your family. Choose your husband first. Work with him, be aligned with him going into this holiday season. Choose a code word so you can support each other on the dinner party battlefield.

If you don't think your husband is ready to be on your team, start praying. Be a prayerful wife and do your best to understand his personality and what he's going through. What an amazing gift it would be to find healing this holiday season!

Marriage is worth fighting for. Finding peace in our marriages is better than just about any other present I can think of.

Holiday Activities

May the ardent light of our Faith
Guide us all to the cradle of the infant,
As in ancient times a brilliant star
Guided the Oriental kings there.
The King of Kings was born in a humble
manger;
O mighty ones of today, proud of your greatness,
It is to your pride that God preaches.
Bow your heads before the Redeemer!
Bow your heads before the Redeemer!

- O Holy Night by Adolphine Adam[vii]

Before we talk about how to successfully interact with the people you love over the holidays, let's first focus on the activities you will choose to participate in this year. One of the easiest ways to spin out of control during November and December is to sign up for too many activities. This happens because we are usually feeling kind and generous, filled with the holiday spirit of giving back and we simply want to help. We want to both volunteer to serve those less fortunate and to celebrate with the people we love.

It doesn't take too long before cookie parties, gingerbread house decorating, work functions, school functions, church functions, neighborhood parties, and volunteering has crammed your schedule! Suddenly the joy you thought you'd have has given way to chaos. Instead of spending time with loved ones, you're spending your time simply driving from one thing to another, throwing fast food at the kids, and feeling stressed out.

Here's an example of how one holiday activity went awry for my family. In October, the local zoo would host "Zoolights" in the evening. Doesn't it sound delightful to walk through the zoo in the twilight with beautiful twinkling lights while holding a cup of warm hot chocolate?

As the event drew near, I became so excited about the upcoming festive opportunities that I rallied some friends and planned a Zoolights trip.

It sounded magical, but here's what really happened. I didn't quite realize that it doesn't get dark until 6 p.m. and my husband was running late from work. I tossed some food at the kids, which they don't eat because they're excited about going to the zoo. We were now late and I felt awful because we were supposed to be meeting a few other families. I was short and stern with the kids, forcing them in the car.

As we pulled up to the zoo, I realized I forgot the hot chocolate and gloves.

The kids were cold and cranky because it's passed their bedtime. The zoo was crowded – seriously, did the entire city come on this one night? I tried to chat with my friends but the two-year-old was melting down. I finally gave in and bought a $5 cup of hot chocolate despite a tight budget.

Suddenly, my chest was tight, no one was having fun, and I felt like a big Zoolights failure. So much for making lovely family memories!

We continue to have similar experiences for many of the activities we sign up for in the months of November and December. They always sound great, but they often devolve into tears, sugar crashing, and mom returning home feeling as if no one grew closer to Jesus or bonded with family as she had envisioned.

Don't fear! This year we are going to be critical and thoughtful about every event we consider signing up for. We may still choose to brave the difficult of an evening Zoolights outing, but we will be crystal clear on our goals for the event, and we'll put some plans in place for making it go more smoothly!

I call this the Remake Your Calendar exercise!

Remake Your Calendar Exercise

Take out a piece of paper and write down every single activity you want to do between November 1st and January 6th (Epiphany). Make sure to include your own family traditions as well.

- Parties (neighborhood, work, church, etc.?)
- Church events
- School events
- Serving at a soup kitchen
- Participating in an Adopt-A-Family drive
- Thanksgiving/Friendsgiving (think of the few days before and after this day as well)
- Christmas (Mass, breakfast, dinner, Christmas Eve., etc.)
- Cookie decorating, gingerbread house decorating
- Putting up your own decorations
- Zoolights, driving around to see Christmas lights, tree lighting ceremony, etc.
- Getting your own Christmas tree and decorating it

After making your list, take out your phone and look at pictures from last year. What else are you missing? Make sure everything is written down.

Now, ask yourself, will you have a peaceful holiday season if you do all those things?

The answer may very well be yes! Maybe you love the hustle and bustle of the holidays and making sweet memories with your children. I have a few friends who think the Christmas season is the best. They are never happier than when they're covered in flour, cooking up a storm, and wrapping presents in the glow of their massively decorated house!

No one can tell you how to celebrate the holidays. This exercise is about being honest with yourself and choosing things with intentionality.

I personally don't like doing more than 1-2 things per week. I don't particularly enjoy doing things after 5 p.m. because I have little children. If there's an evening event that I'd like to attend, I'll first consider if I could find/afford a babysitter for the younger two.

Once you have created your initial list and have put some thought into what events are the most important, discuss your list with your spouse. What are his/her favorite activities? Recall last year especially if it was full of chaos and stress. Emphasize that this year you want to simplify. You may each have to compromise on a few activities, but this process enables both of you to enjoy the events you have chosen together.

Once you've decided what's made the cut and what hasn't, communicate this to your family. I try to make the tough choices early. It's easier to tell someone you're not coming to an event in October before the holiday season begins. It's a lot harder to say no two days before when you realize you're too busy to go. If you wait, you feel guilty for not only canceling but doing so at the last minute.

If you normally visit Zoolights every year, but this year you've decided not to, tell your kids early. Explain to them that you want more quality time as a family this year and less chaos. Maybe you can let them pick out a neat project to do at home instead, like stringing up popcorn for the tree! They will likely be disappointed so it's important that you stay strong.

You are fighting the good fight to live counter-culturally. You are choosing to stand up for your family and say, "No, we will not be busy and stressed out simply because the world tells us to."

Make sure you're leaving enough time for peace and quiet in your home. Make sure you're reading your Bible and helping your kids understand why we celebrate Christmas at all – because of our Lord who became flesh to become a perfect sacrifice for our sins! Always bring the conversation back to eternity because that's what we're really fighting for.

Take control of your life and your calendar this year. Be intentional about the activities that you take on.

Is Advent Penitential?

O come, O come, Emmanuel,
And ransom captive Israel,
That mourns in lonely exile here,
Until the Son of God appear.
Rejoice! Rejoice! Emmanuel
Shall come to thee, O Israel.

- *O Come, O Come, Emmanuel*[viii]

I had been Catholic for a few years before I heard this idea that Advent is a penitential season of the church. This actually made me very happy! Given my bad memories of November and December in my childhood, I let out a huge sigh of relief that I wouldn't have to participate in the loud hubbub of the holidays until December 24th. This seemed like a wonderful excuse to keep the color and noise out of my home.

One year, we completely embraced this idea and had a penitential Advent. We played soft, quiet music sung by nuns. We cut out almost all television and tried to focus on getting ready for Jesus to come. We prayed more, and each gave up something just as we do during Lent. We made food for other families. We put up purple decorations but didn't decorate for Christmas until a few days before Christmas Eve. We lit our Advent candle and put up a Jesse tree. It was quiet and wonderful!

When I geared up to write about how Advent should be penitential, I did some research. To my surprise, even though there were several websites that called out Advent as being penitential, in the end, the Vatican resources (including the Catechism) said otherwise. God bless our Catholic faith for providing a place we can always go to for answers!

Advent is not a penitential season.

It is a season of preparation, but it is not a season for penance. With that in mind, I'd like to suggest that we really focus on Advent as a season of preparation. I still intend to create a peaceful and quiet atmosphere in my home. I want my children to be filled with awe as we wait for the baby Jesus. Just like that first Christmas; waiting, hoping, and praying that the Messiah would come.

We will prepare our home for Christmas by giving away some of our toys and warm clothes. We clean our home and light candles to create a welcome space for Jesus to come. We'll still put up our purple decorations, our Advent wreath, and our Jesse Tree. We'll celebrate the O'Antiphons. We'll talk about the real meaning of Christmas and why Christ coming into the world was such an amazing thing.

It's especially important to talk to our children about the way Jesus came into the world. He wasn't born in a palace. He was born into poverty to teach us detachment from material things. We must cling to this most of all during Christmas. The devil has done an excellent job of getting us to choose materialism to celebrate the least material person that ever lived. That is what the devil does best – he takes something that is good, and he twists it just a little, so it's distorted.

Don't get me wrong, owning things and giving/receiving gifts is not intrinsically wrong but it is easy for us to have a disordered attachment to wealth. This greed, this intense pull for more sparkly things can get us into trouble at a time when we should really be quietly preparing for our Lord in the peace of our own homes.

Protect yourself this year as you step into the glittery scene the world has created in November and December. It's hard to encounter Jesus in a world bedecked with colorful lights and shiny packages. You can't go into any store and avoid the sounds of Christmas music or holiday decorations. It is a battle you will have to fight every time you step out of your house.

Again, none of these things are bad per say, but when we are the victim of a constant onslaught to our senses, we have to put more effort forward to see Jesus in that noise.

It seems like the world has simply decided to party through Advent in anticipation of the secular version of Christmas. To be honest, it's exhausting trying to swim against the current of that energy but oh is it worth it. It is worth everything in this world to have a genuine encounter with Jesus – to have a deep relationship with the God-became-man who walked this Earth, suffered our pain, and wants so desperately to love us. There is no present that can compare.

Bring peace and joy wherever you go this holiday season. Don't be distracted by the lights and the noise. Don't get caught up in the appearances of parties, decorations, and posturing through gifts. Give people your time.

Time is the best gift we can give when it's coupled with love. Give time to Jesus through prayer and give time to the people in your life with genuine love. Let them feel loved and let them feel truly seen. That is what most of us are longing for in this world, genuine connection. Ultimately, each person is longing for a genuine connection with Jesus, but if they have not encountered Him yet, we may have to be Jesus to that someone until they come to meet Him themselves.

Let Advent not only be a time of preparation for Jesus but a time to prepare for eternity in Heaven. What sweeter gift could we desire than this?

Decorate Before December 24th?

Adoramus te Christe,
et benedicimus tibi, poco piu mosso
Quia per sanctam crucem tuam, redemi sti mumdum,
qui passus es pro nobis
Domine miserere Domine
Domine miserere nobis.

- Adoramus Te[ix]

Don't fear! I'm not going to steal your Christmas joy and deny you the tradition of decorating for Christmas after Thanksgiving. I personally feel that to do it before Thanksgiving is really doing it too soon, but there is no Christmas decoration police to catch you!

While you may choose to deck your halls well before December 24th, let me call you first and foremost to decorate with intention. What message do you hope to send by putting up Santas and snowmen before Advent? How will you share the message of the Gospels with those who enter your home?

It is not morally wrong to decorate early (and thoroughly) before Christmas Eve. Though I myself am drawn to a more quiet start to the season, reserving the big decorations and colorful lights for the Twelve Days of

Christmas, there is by no means a hard and fast rule about this.

Again, I would call you to be intentional. I would call you to think of others and ask yourself, how can I decorate this year in a way that serves my family, my community, and my Lord? When that is your mission, your decorations (no matter when they go up) will spread the love of God to others. That is what Christmas is supposed to be about.

Sticky Family Situations

And all the souls on earth shall sing
On Christmas Day, on Christmas Day
And all the souls on earth shall sing
On Christmas Day in the morning

- I Saw Three Ships[x]

Let's talk about our family members. Some of you probably feel tense just thinking about these emotionally charged relationships. Maybe you have a snarky aunt, a disapproving mother, a competitive sister, or a cousin who insists on poking you about your faith. We don't get to pick our family, and often we find ourselves eating next to strong personalities that clash with our own.

You might dread the holidays knowing that harsh words are often exchanged. Perhaps in your family, only fake words are said as issues are swept under the rug or drowned out by glasses of wine. These events truly can be uncomfortable.

If you don't have a difficult family, give thanks to God and move on to the next section of the book. This section is for those of us with messy families. We have come to expect confrontations that slowly siphon the joy out of Christmas – leaving nothing behind but friction.

This year is going to be different. I'm going to give you a few strategies for preventing and managing those yucky moments. This year I want you to feel really confident in handling the difficult members of your family, your office party, or a challenging person you know will be at all the same parties this year.

Remember that Jesus came into the world to teach us to love each other. He proved His love for us in the most amazing way possible – by dying for our sins. Our job is to love the Lord our God and to love our neighbor… and yes, that includes our crazy family members too!

Our goal this year is to have genuine joy! We want to rejoice in Jesus!

Christmas is a time of anticipation – of hope. We want to celebrate this truth as we wait for the savior to come into the world. Let us focus on Him and not let worldly situations and petty people get in the way.

We're going to accomplish this by first going through the Letting It Go exercise on the next page.

Let It All Out Exercise

The first step to defusing family situations is to go through the Let It All Out exercise. You can choose to read through the whole exercise and complete it later, or you can grab a piece of paper right now and do it while you're reading the steps.

I want you to make a list of everyone in your family (or any other charged relationship you know you'll face this holiday season.) Make a list of these people and then write down all the prickly things about them (i.e., they don't respect your faith, they're always trying to one-up you, they drink too much and flirt with you, etc.)

This isn't a list about judgment or anger. Right now we are simply scientists. We are sitting down and writing our observations based on past data. We are stating the facts. Person X has previously said or done Y to me during the holidays.

This list is simply a brainstorming session about the difficult personalities you'll confront and harsh comments you're likely to hear this holiday season. It's better for us to face them now in the comfort of our own home where we feel strong and secure than to be caught off guard over the cookie table.

Here are some characters I'm going to make up for this exercise:

- Mary Jane questions me about homeschooling
- Uncle Joe makes jokes about the weight I've gained
- Dad asks me if I'll ever find a husband
- Cousin Elizabeth will tell me about all the fabulous accomplishments of her children, challenging me to do the same
- Cousin Mark always drinks too much, and it's sad to see his addiction play out
- Grandma Sue will wipe her fingers along the mantle and tell me how dusty it is
- My mother-in-law will make snide comments about my poor cooking

Let's be honest; your family isn't going to be different this year.

If there's an alcoholic in your family, he likely will drink too much again this year. If your mother usually gives more thoughtful presents to your sister, this year will probably be the same.

It's important that we acknowledge these people and the situations we are likely to face early so that, when they come up, we can be more emotionally prepared. Facing awkward or negative situations is easier if we have thought about and prepared for them ahead of time. It won't feel like a surprise. It may still be hurtful, but it probably won't hurt as deeply if we see it coming.

Dig deep during this exercise. You may list some situations that happened in your childhood. While they may not repeat with the same people, the same type of event/conversation might trigger some trauma for you.

> If someone in your family is gay and thinks the Catholic Church hates gay people, he may pick a fight with you every year – write that down.
>
> If you have a parent who, no matter what you do, is always disappointed in you – write that down.
>
> If you were made fun of for wearing a goofy outfit when you were a child, you might be extra self-conscious about what you wear and what people say about your clothes – write that down.
>
> If you have a grandparent who is a little out of touch with reality and you bet she is going to give you your fifteenth, hand-made, lace doily – write that down.

The point of this exercise is that our families are not likely to have changed this year. They're going to be the same people, struggling with the same crosses. It would be naive of us to think that somehow, this year, Thanksgiving is going to be lovely and all the past problems will be gone.

Having reasonable expectations will help us curb our anxiety. We will feel calmer and ready to deal with the confrontations we expect to arise. We will feel empowered to deal with the people we're going to have to face.

When you're finished, take a moment and look at the list.

Look at all the ugly things you wrote down. Look at all the yuckiness, hurt feelings, and brokenness of the people on that list. Now I want you to tell yourself, "This is not my fault."

It's important that you say it out loud. Look at those names and say, "This is not my fault."

You are not responsible for what's on that piece of paper. You can love these people, you can pray for them, but you need to let go of any guilt you feel about their behavior. What they're dealing with, the crosses that they carry, and the state of their heart is not your fault.

You are not God.

You are not in charge of other people's lives.

What we are in charge of and responsible for is how we speak to people. When we speak out of anger or spite, we are wrong, and we should apologize. We do not need to apologize, however, for the choices our family makes.

We all need Jesus and, when we live a life that's turned away from Him, we experience deep pain. We get stuck in ruts – making bad choices and living toxic lives. We all do this on some level. Some of us turn away from Him in small moments each day. Some of us have turned away from Him for years.

If you have a family member who has turned away from God, either in a big or small way, it is not your fault.

God gives each person the freewill, the choice to follow Him. You are not responsible if others reject Him.

One of the reasons these holiday confrontations are so difficult is because we care deeply about our friends and our family. The more we love them, the more we care about their choices and their opinions of us. The more we love someone, the more their faults seem to hurt us and the more we are aware of our own faults.

When we love people, it makes us vulnerable, and their words can cut us more deeply. By going through the Letting It Go exercise, you are acknowledging their pain and the pain you've experienced in the past. You are staring at it objectively, like a scientist, telling your brain, "This is not my fault. I am not responsible for their behavior."

Our hope is that we can prevent or at least short-circuit our strong feelings of pain, anger, and sadness when these situations come up. Again, we already know they are likely situations so it makes sense that we should be prepared for them.

Once we have the list of sticky situations we might encounter, we release ourselves from feeling responsible for other people's actions, we now look to Mary for healing.

Give Them To Mary

I have traveled many moonless nights
Cold and weary with a babe inside
And I wonder what I've done
Holy father you have come
And chosen me now to carry your son

- Breath of Heaven (Mary's Song) by Amy Grant[xi]

I converted to Catholicism in my adulthood after a few years of being a Protestant. I wasn't raised with the idea of praying to Mary or "giving" people to her. I was fortunate that a few years after becoming Catholic, someone recommended the *33 Days to Morning Glory*[xii], an at-home retreat program. You read a few pages out of a book and then fill in a few worksheet questions each day for 33 days. At the end of the program, you take your consecration vows and consecrate yourself to Jesus through Mary.

Through consecration, you give all your good works and sacrifices to Mary. She then presents them to her son. They are amplified by her presentation – like a queen who takes your meager offering of a piece of fruit and presents it to the king on a golden platter. Throughout the program, you learn about Mary's great love for us as her children.

The book shares stories of some saints who entrusted their family members to Mary. Some of the family members converted a great gift from Mary. Others never converted (at least publically), but these saints experienced deep peace by offering their family to Mary. The Saints trusted the Blessed Mother to care for their family members. It relieved these saints of having to worry about their non-Catholic family.

After we acknowledge that we can't control our family or change their decisions in the Letting It Go exercise, we can find great peace by asking our Blessed Mother to watch over them. This doesn't mean they won't experience pain or hardship – instead, we ask her to pray for their salvation. God does not promise us a life without suffering, but He does promise that all our suffering can lead to eternity in the Kingdom of Heaven.

We trust that by asking for her intercession, she will fight for their souls.

I enjoy reading stories of people who, after getting to Heaven, are told by the Lord that they only earned salvation because of Mary's intercession. Most of these stories are hard to verify (especially those that don't have an imprimatur from the Vatican), so we don't always know if these stories are true. Still, plenty of the saints have talked about the incredible intercessory power that Mary has.

I was pretty skeptical while going through the 33 Days program. I did not expect that I would find the peace the book had promised. But somewhere on the journey, Mary wiggled her way into my heart. She helped me to let go of my fears and my need to control everything. She allowed me to give my family up to her. It really did change my life.

I found an amazing peace after I asked our Blessed Mother to care for my family. I asked her to care for my husband, my children, and all the members of my family. I handed them over to her care, along with my trust.

My sinfulness and selfishness will always get in the way of my ability to make perfect decisions, but that's not true of Mary. When you give your family to Mary, two things will happen. First, she will care for your family and love them with the heart of a perfect mother. She will never stop thinking about them. She will return to her son over and over again and say, "Son, I love this person. Please take care of them."

Second, she will take the weight of responsibility of your family off of your shoulders. I used to feel so worried about my family. I felt responsible for all of them. Few of them are religious, none of them are Catholic, and many of them struggle financially or have serious health issues.

I used to lay in bed at night, and I would just worry about them. "Lord, what am I going to do? How am I going to take care of all of these people?"

My heart would break for them. I love my dad very much, and we're close. Yet this man, who I admire so much, he doesn't believe in Jesus. He went to Catholic school, had a horrible experience, and now he doesn't believe in organized religion.

How often I used to lift my face up to the Lord and ask, "Lord, how is my dad going to be saved? How could I possibly be happy in Heaven without him?"

This used to weigh heavily on my heart before I went through Marian consecration. But after my consecration, I gave them all to Mary, and I said, "Mama Mary, here. You take my daddy, and you pray for him. You change his heart. You take my husband, and you lead him to Heaven, I'll follow you. You take my children, guide them even after I'm gone."

What's so special about Mary is that she gives you the grace to absolutely believe that she's going to take care of the people you entrust her with.

I'm not lying or making it up; I genuinely don't worry about my dad's salvation anymore. I don't worry about my mom who suffers from chronic pain. I've given her to Mary, and I know Mary will care for her. I don't know what that's going to look like, and I don't know what that's going to mean, but it's not on me anymore.

If you haven't gone through Marian consecration, I highly suggest that you make time to do it. If you have the chance to do the 33 Days to Morning Glory program with a group, do it. It is an absolutely life-changing process. This year I'm going to go through the older version called True Devotion by St. Louis de Montfort[xiii], which I have been told is a more intense version of the 33 Days to Morning Glory program. I'm looking forward to deepening my relationship with our Blessed Mother.

I want you to give every single person in your family to Mary. Do this out loud, one by one. Name them as you entrust them to her. If you can do this in an Adoration Chapel, that's even better!

No prayer is too big for our Blessed Mother. She is the Queen of Heaven. She is the spouse of the Holy Spirit. She is the mother of Jesus, and He loves her so much that He made her the Mediatrix of All Grace. This Advent Season, if you don't know why she has all of these titles, then your homework is to go discover the many names and powers of Mary.

I want you to let go of your worry and your anxiety about your family. To find peace, we have to let go of the things God never asked us to carry. We have to make room for Him to come and change our hearts and ultimately our souls. It's hard for Him to bring us peace when we're busy worrying about things we cannot control.

Role Play Likely Scenarios Exercise

The next thing I want you to do is to find a trusted friend or family member and role-play some of the yucky or uncomfortable conversations you think are going to come up this year. If a family member usually challenges you about why your kids aren't in Catholic school, they're probably going to poke you about that again this year. Be prepared for that conversation.

Choose how you're going to respond. You can either defend your choices with a few points that you've lovingly prepared, or you can say, "You know what, it's the holidays. I don't want to get into that right now. Shoot me an email, and I'd be happy to talk with you about that later."

We don't have to always verbally defend our faith, preach about what we believe, or discuss the reasons behind our life choices. It's important that we know our faith well and that we live our lives with intention, but Thanksgiving isn't always the best time for a lecture. You are not obligated to explain yourself.

Make a choice about how you're going to respond to these situations in advance; it's very likely that they're going to come up. You can decrease your anxiety by having a plan and rehearsing it. This can help you feel empowered when going into situations you're normally nervous about.

We know these emotionally-charged situations are likely to make us feel either angry or bad about ourselves. In order to avoid that, let's have more control over our emotions. Roleplay likely situations so can practice that self-control. Even though you're just acting, it won't be difficult to call up those real and ugly feelings you know you're going to experience.

One of the lies the devil has sold to modern society is that we cannot control our emotional reactions. You are allowed to feel and say whatever you want – it's healthy! If you want to be angry, that's okay. If you want to yell at people, that's fine.

This is a lie.

We don't get to choose what happens to us or what people say to us, but we do get to choose how we respond. Nobody has the power to *make* you angry. You always have a choice to react in anger as a response to an injustice that has happened to you.

Many of us are also confused about anger because anger is so directly tied to sadness. When our parents question something we're doing, we might react in anger. Often, however, what we're really feeling deep down is a rejection by our parents – whom we love so much. Although this feeling is really rooted in sadness, we often react with an angry response.

Again, your parent's actions are not your fault, and they are not your responsibility. People can pick on you, insult you, bully you, and even try to make you angry but you always get to choose how you respond.

It is your choice what emotion you respond with when someone backs you into a corner. Instead of allowing your chest to get tight, feeling trapped, and saying something you might regret later, have a plan.

Knowing what you're going to say will help you stay calm. Even if you love this person, and even if you strongly disagree with what they're saying, you don't have to let their words increase your blood pressure. You don't have to let them create tension in your body. Take a deep breath and know that you already have a plan about what you're going to say. You're going to be a lot less anxious this year.

Decorations

He rules the world with truth and grace,
And makes the nations prove
The glories of his righteousness,
And wonders of his love,
And wonders of his love,
And wonders, wonders, of his love.

- Joy to the World by Isaac Watts

Confession time: I have a real problem in the decorations department. Well, the truth is I used to have a real problem with decorations, but I'm a lot better about it now. I would like to formally go on record and blame the Pottery Barn catalog for my decorations problem.

I don't even subscribe to the Pottery Barn catalog and yet, somehow, every year for at least the last ten years, I end up stumbling upon a Pottery Barn catalog during the holiday season. Suddenly I'm flipping through the beautiful pages of glittery pumpkins, snowy white owls, and the most lovely (and yet understated) Christmas decorations.

It looks like a magical dinner party that I would discover if I traveled through a wardrobe.

I suddenly have a deep desire to make my house look like that. I've never had a lot of money to blow on decorations though so after I set down that Pottery Barn catalog, I would head to the Dollar Store or a thrift store. I would buy a couple of things, put them up in my home, and then stand back and look at them.

It looked like a seven-year-old decorated my house for the holidays. I would look back at the catalog and see a huge disconnect. Upon seeing this great disparity, I would feel sad or upset. I remember my husband came home one day and I verbally pounced on him as soon as he came through the door. "Michael! Why can't I just make my house look like a home? Why can't I get this right? I'm adult. I should be able to decorate my house and have it look nice, but it just looks stupid!"

There might have even been a foot stomp or two in that ranting speech.

My, how ungrateful I sound, but I think many women can sympathize with these feelings. We want so desperately to create a beautiful and calm atmosphere at home, and yet so many of us completely lack the skills to do so with ease and grace… and without a huge budget!

Were there holiday decorating classes we missed somewhere along the way?

While it's not a good idea to throw a tantrum about poorly coordinating decorations, we often feel justified in our disappointment. I'm quite sure we all have at least one friend who is naturally gifted in this way. Her decorations are beautiful, perfectly proportioned, inviting, and warm. "How does she do that?" we wonder quietly to ourselves.

But you see, God doesn't promise us all the same talents. He gives each of us very specific talents to help us on our path to sainthood. Your friend may have a natural eye for good design. You may be superb at reading out loud to your children or a fantastic budget keeper.

The brilliance of the devil is that he always takes something good and twists it. Women were designed to be receivers. We receive people into our homes, we receive children into our hearts, and we are often healers in the Church receiving pain and complaints. We offer up prayers along with hugs and service. We care for those around us. It's natural for us to do so.

Even if a woman doesn't have any biological children, she was made to be a spiritual mother to someone. That is part of the essence of womanhood. That is the reason women want their homes to be warm and inviting. They want people to feel welcome and to have a comfortable time at their house.

This is a good and pure intention, but the devil twists it. He whispers in your ear that you're a failure if you don't have a beautiful house with Pottery Barn decorations. People aren't going to be happy if your silverware and your glasses don't match. People won't feel welcome if you don't serve gourmet food with lovely garnishes.

As the holiday season approaches, many of us are already feeling anxious about the idea of people coming into our houses. We want them to feel comfortable, but we're a little confused about what really matters. What is the minimum level of decorations and food coordination required to make people feel at home?

It's silly that we worry so much about the state of our own home when I'm quite certain we don't think twice about the state of someone else's home.

I can't think of one single time when I've been at a friend's house and thought, "Oh friend, your decorations are not very pretty. I don't feel very welcome here. That food would look better if it was placed on a prettier platter. I see that you didn't dust behind your television – it's awfully dusty back there."

Those thoughts have never crossed my mind so why am I so worried about another woman passing these unlikely judgments on my own event?

Friends, we have done this to ourselves. We perpetuate this myth that our houses must be glittering and perfect before we can have people over. We scramble to make things look nice, often trampling our own family in the process. Pinterest isn't helping at all. With it, you can type in "Christmas decorations" and see the best of the best presented in a colorful grid.

It can feel like everyone else is getting this right – everyone except me.

This year I want you to let go of your perfectionist tendencies about decorating your home and having guests over. Jesus doesn't care about the coordination of your wall hangings. He is looking at the state of your heart.

I'm not saying that decorating is bad. If you can decorate without becoming stressed or being unkind to your family, go for it! I have a few decorations I put up every year that I really enjoy. I like creating a festive atmosphere and celebrating the changing seasons.

What I don't do anymore is let the urge to decorate competitively…dominate me. I don't get upset at my husband or annoyed with my children because I'm focused on making our home look like a catalog. I don't have deep envy when I see somebody else's decorations. I'm no longer letting this topic touch my heart and my soul.

Creating beauty in your world is not a bad thing – but when you do it by sacrificing your peace, it's not okay. So this year, when you are thinking about decorating or planning a party and bringing people into your home, remember that Jesus made women to receive people. Give them love and show them the light of Christ.

Ask for help, "Jesus, help me make this event about you and not about me."

Gift Giving

Go tell it on the mountain,
over the hills and everywhere;
go tell it on the mountain,
that Jesus Christ *is born.*

\- *Go Tell It On The Mountain*[xiv]

Most of the problems mentioned so far can be solved by managing expectations, either yours or those of your friends and family. Expectation management is equally as crucial when it comes to finding a balance about gifts.

If you haven't yet, sit down with your spouse and get on the same page about gift expectations for your nuclear family and then for your extended family. Plan the gifts you intend to give this year, not only to each other but to the rest of your friends and family.

I am a huge fan of Dave Ramsey. He would definitely say it is not okay to use debt to buy Christmas presents – and I agree with this wholeheartedly. If you don't have enough money this year, instead of overextending yourself and filling up your credit cards to make a good impression, stop and ask yourself, "Why am I doing this?"

Imagine that Jesus is walking through the mall with you. You have to look Him in the eye and say, "I know I don't have the money for it, but I just want to make my little girl happy, so I'm going to buy her this doll anyway."

Can you do say that without flinching?

I'm pretty sure Jesus would tell you that what your daughter really wants is your love. Sure, children always enjoy presents, but not at the cost of parents becoming stressed and upset about bills. Children most want genuine warmth, love, and quality time. You can often make them happy with handmade, inexpensive gifts and genuine quality time.

Looking back, I think my sadness about not receiving a lot of gifts would have been greatly minimized if my parents had spent quality time with me during the holidays. We could have made presents or played board games. Instead, it was the bad combination of busy work schedules *and* no presents that made it so difficult.

If you have an extended family that pressures you to buy presents, then you need to communicate new expectations to them this year.

Send out an email before Thanksgiving and say:

> "Hey guys, I love you so much! I'm excited to spend the holiday season with you this year. I just wanted to let you know in advance that my husband and I are really trying to pay off debt (or save money for a house). Money is pretty tight, and we're not going to spend a lot on presents this year. I wanted to let you know that ahead of time so there are no hurt feelings."

Maybe you can choose to give out handmade things or coupons for service (e.g., good for a free back massage, raking up leaves, etc.) Make a plan and communicate it clearly. I want you to manage the expectations of the other people in your family by letting them know ahead of time what you're going to do.

If you're going to do something drastically different this year in your own family, you should also let them know. Sit down and communicate the changes to your kids, so they're not surprised and disappointed this Christmas.

> "Hey kiddos, we love you so much! This year we're focusing on some big financial goals. God has asked us to be good stewards of our money, so we're working hard to pay off debt or save for a house. Christmas is going to be simpler this year. We're going to do handmade presents and fewer presents for each of you. Thank you for having a good attitude and supporting our family. We're all working hard to do this together! There are other ways we will make Christmas special this year, and we're going to spend a lot of time together as a family."

Don't be scared to have this conversation. Remember, you are raising children to be good stewards of their own money in the future. Even if you've messed it up until right now, it's not too late to start communicating good financial choices to your kids. If you have to make sacrifices, that's okay. Explain to them how you got into this pickle and why you're going to work hard to get out of it. What a great life lesson!

Taking responsibility is something we want to teach our children. Showing them that we can make good choices in the face of American culture that tells us to simply put it on a credit card and pay it later, will make them strong when they have to do their own Christmas battle.

I want you to feel proud of yourself and your decisions. I want you to feel responsible. You will hit January feeling on top of your budget instead of saddled with debt wondering how you let it get so out of control. It can be so satisfying!

Envy and Jealousy

Said the shepherd boy to the mighty king,
do you know what I know
In your palace warm, mighty king,
do you know what I know
A Child, a Child shivers in the cold
Let us bring Him silver and gold
Let us bring Him silver and gold

- Do You Hear What I Hear? By Noel Regney[xv]

Envy and jealousy are words that are often used interchangeably – I think for most people they mean basically the same thing. In truth, these words mean very different things but I believe our casual American language has smashed them together to mean "I want what she has." Now whether you want that thing simply because you'd like to have it or whether you believe it should be rightfully yours and not hers, it's still a yucky feeling that's likely robbing you of your peace.

I do want to define these terms for you, however, so you can educate yourself about the difference and hopefully protect yourself from giving in to either of these feelings.

Before we dive into these two words, I want first to explain that feelings themselves are not sinful. Let's use lust as an example. If a man passes by a pretty woman and his eye notices that she is sexy, that initial feeling is not sinful. If he continues to stare at her or daydreams about her throughout the day, then these feelings have now become sinful. If he seeks her out and has an affair with her, it's a mortal sin.

Many of us will have fleeting feelings of envy and jealousy that pop up. This is quite normal. We don't, however, have to dwell on these feelings or act on these feelings. Giving in to feelings of envy and jealousy can lead to venial or even mortal sin.

Let's learn about the difference between envy and jealousy so we can more clearly spot them when they pop up!

Envy

I wonder as I wander out under the sky,
How Jesus the Savior did come for to die.
For poor on'ry people like you and like I...
I wonder as I wander out under the sky.

- I Wonder As I Wander by John Jacob Niles[xvi]

Envy is defined in the catechism as "sadness at the sight of another's goods and the immoderate desire to acquire them for oneself, even unjustly." (CCC 2539).

The quick feeling of envy is not immediately a sin. I often see a mom with a big backyard, and I think, "Oh, I wish we had a big backyard." This is a momentary feeling of sadness at seeing another's goods. If I give into this feeling and dwell on it, letting it rob me of my peace, it can become a venial sin. Maybe I spend two hours on Zillow looking at houses and wishing we could afford to move.

If I make snarky comments to a friend about how the Jones family doesn't deserve their nice backyard because they're mean people, now this envy has become a venial sin. If I act on these feelings and cause harm to the person who has what I want or if I commit a crime to obtain it for myself, now it's a mortal sin.

If I purchased a house, I couldn't afford and put my family in financial danger just so could I get what I wanted; this would also be sinful. An easier example to understand would be if I wanted a nice purse but I didn't have the money to purchase it, so I stole it. This would be a mortal sin.

Most of us simply see what someone else has, and we want it too. We aren't happy with what God has given us, and we want more.

"Envy represents a form of sadness and therefore a refusal of charity; the baptized person should struggle against it by exercising good will. Envy often comes from pride; the baptized person should train himself to live in humility." (CCC 2540)

One of the best ways to combat envy is to focus on humility and gratitude. Post the Litany of Humility somewhere in your home and say it often. It's amazing how quickly it helps me to get off my high horse and to stop feeling sorry for myself about the things I don't have. I try to immediately give praise to God for His amazing gifts and His incredible sacrifice for my sins.

As I'll mention later, keeping a gratitude journal is also a great way to avoid or overcome feelings of envy. When we focus on our blessings, we fill our hearts with gratitude, so there is no more room for desiring what someone else has. This is what we should always seek to do because God has blessed us tremendously and we ought to turn around and give Him thanks for these blessings.

As I did some more research, I found several other phrases about and definitions of envy:

- To want what someone else has
- Discontented longing for someone else's advantages
- Anger turned inward for something someone else has (e.g., status, possessions, power, wealth, etc.)

It sounds terrible, but most of us are more envious than we wish to admit. Even if we don't wish to take away from another person, we have far too strong a desire for their good things. I have a feeling that when most of us say we are jealous of someone, we're really just envious of them. We don't want to take away their good things; we just want them too.

This feeling is dangerous though because it can quickly escalate into sinful behavior. We're basically telling God that what we have is not enough and that we are not happy. We aren't content, and we lack peace.

It's common to struggle with envy and for these feelings to pop up, but we don't have to dwell on these feelings. We don't have to give in to them and wallow in our wanting. Our flesh is sinful and weak. God knows this about us, and His mercy is endless.

The important part is to push those feelings away and ask for God's forgiveness that you stopped being content with what He's given to you. He will always forgive you, and He will always extend His mercy to you.

If you struggle with this, I highly recommend Elizabeth Scalia's book *Little Sins Mean A Lot*[xvii]. She talks about how quickly little sins like gossip or jealousy can spiral out of control until they are big, yucky sins.

When you experience feelings of envy, take them to the Lord. Don't give in to them and certainly don't commit sin to acquire things you wish you had.

Jealousy

O star of wonder, star of night,
Star with royal beauty bright,
Westward leading, still proceeding,
Guide us to thy perfect light.

- *We Three Kings by John Henry Hopkins*[xviii]

Jealousy, by contrast, is to want a good thing that someone else has that you feel ought to be yours. A common example is when someone is flirting with your husband. He is *your* husband, and you feel that his attention should be on you and not the woman he is talking to. You are jealous that he is smiling at her.

Perhaps you were passed over for a promotion, and you're upset that your co-worker got it instead of you. Technically, it wasn't yours, to begin with, but if you perceived that it was rightfully yours, you would feel jealous and wish that person hadn't gotten it instead of you.

We can be jealous in our friendships too. If a particular mom is very popular in your playgroup because she dresses well and is funny, you may be jealous of her. It's not that you want her clothes. Rather, you wish the other moms didn't like her so much so they might like you more.

Here are some other phrases that also describe jealousy:

- Worried someone will take what you have
- Possessively suspicious
- Apprehensive of rivalry
- Resentment of a rival or person who has been more successful and is competing with you

Here is another example of envy and jealousy.

Example of jealousy:

You're at a dinner party, and your husband admires your friend's decorations, you are jealous of the attention he is giving. You wish he noticed how hard you worked to decorate your house. This desire isn't necessarily sinful – your husband is supposed to cherish and treasure you. It can become sinful if you stew in anger over those feelings or treat your husband poorly in response.

Example of envy:

You see your friend's beautifully decorated house. You have a fleeting feeling of envy, and you wish you had beautiful decorations. Then this feeling turns sinful. Knowing how badly she manages her finances and marriage, you think she doesn't deserve to have such beautiful decorations. You are probably upset that she made that irresponsible choice. You may even look for subtle ways to discredit her efforts.

One last note about jealousy. There is a good and righteous form of jealousy. God describes Himself as jealous (see Exodus 34:14, Deuteronomy 6:15, and CCC 584) but never as envious. We are all called to desire holiness. It is okay to want good marriages, happy families, and warm, inviting homes. If you see an elderly married couple who is happy, it might inspire you to seek out a good Catholic husband so you too could have a marriage like this. A holy jealousy both wants the good thing for oneself and celebrates the friend that currently has it.

I believe that we experience this type of jealousy as rarely as we experience true righteous anger. I think it's safe to assume that when we have feelings of jealous pop-up, they're not the righteous kind.

When you fall into jealousy, ask God for mercy and forgiveness to help you move on! Now that we've tackled the green-eyed monster let's move on to greed.

"Controlling Your Wanter"

Enough for Him, whom cherubim
Worship night and day,
A breastful of milk,
And a manger full of hay;
Enough for Him, whom angels
Fall down before,
The ox and ass and camel
Which adore.

- *In The Bleak Midwinter by Christina Rossetti*[xix]

Rarely do I consciously wish something good away from someone else. When I see that someone has something I want, I just wish I had it too. I think that's what most of us feel. We just wish we had… more. It's so easy for us to see what we don't have… what we lack and to feel like we're missing out as if life would be better if we had this one more thing.

When these feelings wash over me – when I struggle with envy, it's not the initial thought that is bad. The problem comes when I hold on to these thoughts and feelings for far too long. I chew on them. I let them stew.

I will allow a quick feeling of "I wish I had that" to turn into "I'll never have….." "Why don't I ever get…." "I'm never going to have…"

Because I grew up with little money, it's very easy for me to be dazzled by wealth. I don't tend to want flashy status symbols like a Ferrari or a coach purse, but I do long for the security of a big savings account and luxuries for my children (e.g., piano lessons, sporting equipment, and passes to the museum).

This predilection was developed during my childhood. Although my mom worked really hard to get me into a good school, we didn't have a lot of money. I was able to join a special program for advanced students, which was an amazing opportunity. The difference, though, between the other kids in this great program and me was that they had parents who were doctors, lawyers, or other prestigious positions.

Most of the kids in my class had a lot more money and opportunities than I did. I never felt this disparity more than right after Christmas break. Inevitably, students talked about what they got for Christmas. While they had a long list of glitzy things, I often had nothing interesting to share. I felt embarrassed and ashamed.

There really is no way to get out of answering the question, "What did you get for Christmas?"

That sad 10-year-old girl still lives inside my head. She wants to put her face down, stare at the carpet, and become invisible, so she doesn't have to explain why, even to this day, she gets very little at Christmas. Now, of course, I'm older, and I can see the true and real meaning of Christmas.

I'm thankful that I get to focus on praising Jesus and bringing joy to my family. I work hard to help my kids focus on what truly matters. This doesn't come naturally for children, though. Kids come with a built-in sense of wanting more good things. It's our job to channel that in healthy directions.

In our house, we study the virtues using the We Choose Virtues[xx] program. One of the virtues is contentment, and the catch-phrase for this virtue is "I am content. I control my wanter." It's a cute little phrase that helps children to understand that it's natural for us to want things but that we get to control our wanter. We don't have to give in to it or have bad attitudes when we don't get what we want.

I still have to fight the vice of giving in to envious thoughts around the holidays. I'm envious of people's beautiful homes, their warm, loving families, an abundance of presents, and the special activities people can afford to do with their kids. While this is a struggle of mine, it certainly doesn't mean I need to give into it. It's an ugly feeling, and I don't want it.

The devil, however, still tempts me to compare. That's the tricky thing about the devil – he targets our weaknesses. He doesn't ever tempt me with shoplifting. There's nothing he could whisper in my ear that would get me to steal something from the mall. Instead, he whispers, "Look at how well dressed her children are. Don't you wish you had the money to buy cute clothes for your kids? Why doesn't your husband give you gifts like that? Why isn't your house decorated well for the holidays? Don't you wish you had a beautiful chandelier like that?"

When I was younger, I would let these lies affect me. I would spiral down into a negative, self-talk conversation and then I'd feel deeply depressed about myself. It's too easy to go from, "That scarf is beautiful," to "I'm worthless, and I'll never be happy." This is especially true without Jesus.

But we don't have to live like this!

There are two things I do to battle these ugly thoughts: squish my envy bug and give thanks!

Squish Your Envy Bug Exercise

When envy slips into my mind, I immediately call it out for what it is. "Whoa, that's envy." Then I picture that this envious thought is being whispered in my ear by a little envy bug. It's buzzing around my shoulder saying, "Look at her beautiful and perfectly matched jewelry. You have cheap earrings from Target, and they don't even match your shoes. I bet her wonderful husband bought those for her."

Wow, that sounds really ugly.

That's the thing about envy bugs, though. They're disgusting little creatures who say the ugliest things. We never have to give in to what the envy bug says. To combat this message, I do something physical. I actually take the nail of my pointer finger and press it into my thumb. I imagine I'm squishing this envy bug - splat!

What? You squish a fake bug between your fingers?

Yes, that's exactly what I do, and you know what? It helps! I find that this physical reminder helps me push the thought aside, and then I move on to the next step.

Give Thanks Exercise

Love and joy come to you,
And to you your wassail too;
And God bless you and send you a Happy New Year
And God send you a Happy New Year.

- *Here We Come A-wassailing*[xxi]

Whenever I catch myself thinking jealous or envious thoughts, I immediately give thanks to God. "Lord, thank you for giving Mary Jane the talent of decoration," or "Bless John for being such a good husband to Sue." When we see other people's success, we know it comes from God so thank Him for His blessings. Say a prayer that your friends continue to be blessed. This helps us to anchor our thoughts in Christ and to see His goodness in the world.

We should be grateful for what we have, but we can also be grateful for others. I find that the more gratitude I express, even for the success of those around me, the more peace I have.

When I feel myself getting pouty about what I don't have, I start thinking about all the things that I'm grateful for – my wonderful husband, my healthy children, my home, our food, and all my family who loves me. In America, we are blessed beyond our understanding with everyday luxuries that the rest of the world goes without - not to mention the basic necessities we enjoy that so few countries do.

How many times have you previously heard about the power of gratitude? How often have you read that you should have a gratitude journal that you write in every single day? Do you have one?

Do you actually write down what you're grateful for?

This is such a simple thing, but it really is incredibly powerful. Go get a notebook and just start writing. Write the little things, the big things, the silly things, and all the things that warm your heart. There are literally thousands of things you can be grateful for, and the more you focus on them, the more your mood will improve.

Jesus wants us to recognize that He has given us everything, including our very lives. The fact that we woke up breathing this morning is a gift. We must always turn around and give Him thanks, in every mood and moment. Do this with your whole heart, so there's no room for any of those yucky thoughts.

Squish your envy bug and choose to be grateful. Those two strategies will go a long way in helping you avoid anxiety and depression this holiday season.

Unique Crosses

Midnight, Christians, is the solemn hour,
When God as man descended unto us
To erase the stain of original sin
And to end the wrath of His Father.
The entire world thrills with hope
On this night that gives it a Saviour.
People, kneel down, await your deliverance.
Christmas, Christmas, here is the Redeemer,
Christmas, Christmas, here is the Redeemer! |

- Oh Holy Night by Adolphe Adam[xxii]

When we're dealing with jealousy and envy, we are usually looking at someone else's good fortune, wishing we had it. But it's important that we don't see people for the things they own or the relationships they have. We must see people as souls. And every soul on Earth bears different crosses.

Most of the crosses we bear are invisible. When you're looking at your neighbor across the street, and you're thinking, "How can she afford such a beautiful car?" you may not see that she's really struggling with her marriage. You can't see if she has a horrible relationship with her mother or maybe her children are doing poorly in school.

We all have crosses, and Jesus designed them specifically for us. I couldn't handle your crosses, and you couldn't handle mine. So when you catch yourself looking at someone's life and wishing that you had the things that they have, I want you to stop for a moment and realize that you may not know what you're asking for. To have that person's life means you'd also have their crosses. Not only did Jesus very specifically give us the blessings that we have but He gave us our crosses very purposefully.

I really struggle with insomnia. I have for most of my life. It's difficult for me to both fall asleep and stay asleep. I've been to a lot of doctors with little help, and it remains a cross that I must bear. Some people ask me, "How do you make it on so little sleep? How do you have any energy when you only slept four hours last night?"

It's a good question! The truth is that it is hard. I am often tired. But this is the cross that Jesus gave me. Thankfully I know that He also gave me enough strength and grace to get through it. He gave me this cross because He knew I could handle it.

When you're looking at the people around you feeling jealous of their life, I want you to pause for a moment and recognize that Jesus has designed your life *just for you.* He wants so dearly for you to get into Heaven. He created this very complex equation and said, "I'm going to give you this particular set of virtues and graces to combat your particular struggles. If you live and walk with me, your life will come together. You will get to heaven."

That's what our goal is. It's what we should want more than anything else. It's what we should want for each other too. The more we become like Jesus, the more we want everyone in the world to get to heaven.

When you start thinking of people as special, God-created souls, it's a lot harder to dislike them. When we see people as souls, we want them to get to Heaven too! Who would wish an eternity of hell on anyone? When we focus on each other as souls, we become more patient, more loving, and more like Jesus. This isn't easy, but it's something we have to try to do every day. We have to wake up and say, "I didn't do a good enough job yesterday. Today I'm going to try harder. I'm going to be better."

As the holidays set in and the world starts making more noise, we're going to face an onslaught of music, advertisements, flashing signs, decorations, and lights. It can be so overwhelming that we forget who we are - we forget our mission. We start to drown in the people and the noise, and we stop thinking about Jesus. We stop viewing each other as souls, and we sacrifice eternity for the shallow trinkets in front of us.

You and I are not going to fall for that lie this year. We're going to grab onto genuine joy. We're going to focus on having a simpler, quieter holiday season this year. We're going to block out the noise of the world, and we're going to stare at Jesus. The holidays are when we have to fight the hardest to maintain simplicity. This year I'm hoping to convince a whole bunch of people (myself included) that we don't need to have a big, loud, glitzy Christmas. We don't need to give into all that. We don't need to do what the world tells us will make us happy. We don't need to buy more things or go to every event on the calendar.

We need to connect with Christ. We need to love the people around us. We need to cultivate peace.

If you're struggling this holiday season with a cross, I want you to remember what St. Sebastian said about suffering:

"You will never regret having suffered. Rather, you will regret having suffered so little and suffered that little so badly."

I'm not trying to minimize what you're going through. Instead, I'm trying to get you to see it through the eyes of the Lord. He loves you more than you could ever imagine; this cross He's given you, He's chosen it out of love. He's chosen it because you might need to go through a little pain on Earth in order to spend eternity filled with joy.

I'm so guilty of suffering my crosses badly, especially the small ones. I throw a fit; I pout, I cry out, "Why me Lord? It's not fair!" I lose my peace to ingratitude.

I know better. Instead of waking up and saying, "Jesus why did you give me four little children and expect me to care for them on four hours of sleep?" Now I know that I don't need to hear an answer from Him. I know that God loves me.

I know that He gave me this particular suffering to forge me into someone that's going to be with Him forever. What greater love is there than that?

Forever.

I try to embrace my suffering, and I thank Jesus for my cross because it's this cross that's going to get me to Heaven. I hope my children watch me carry my cross with grace. I hope I inspire them to carry their own crosses because I want nothing more than to spend Heaven with them as well.

This holiday season I want you to focus on finding genuine Joy through trying to be more like Jesus. I know I keep saying this over and over again, but I think we need to keep hearing it. I'm going to get busy later today, and I'm going to forget about Him. I'm going to start making dinner; I'm going to think about cleaning dishes and folding the laundry. I'm going to recall that Thank You card I haven't written yet.

I don't want to get caught up in those things and forget that my day is supposed to be about Christ.

Always Christ.

Loneliness

By thine own eternal Spirit
Rule in all our hearts alone
By thine all sufficient merit
Raise us to thy glorious throne.

- Come, Though Long-Expected Jesus by Christian Friedrich Witt[cxiii]

For many people, the holidays can be a time that highlights loneliness. Perhaps you are single. Perhaps this is the first holiday season after the death of a loved one. Perhaps you've moved away, and you're far from your family this year.

There are many reasons why a normally cheerful season can suddenly feel dark and gloomy. We're nervous about showing up alone to holiday parties. We feel the weight of waking up by ourselves on Christmas morning.

I remember in college feeling really left out around the holidays. I lived several hours away from my family, and I wasn't dating anyone. I would sit in my apartment alone and, at the time, without the comfort that Jesus can bring.

The more I watched Hollywood's versions of Christmas and Hallmark versions of holiday romance, the more I felt completely alone. Even though this is a common place to be at twenty, I felt like I was the only one.

It's also entirely possible to be surrounded by people and to feel completely alone. Sometimes what we really feel is that we are unseen… we are unloved. It can be easy to slap on a pretty dress and a bright smile and play a role at a party. We can laugh and tell stories and seem perfectly fine all the while, deep down, we feel wretched.

We feel as if no one would love us if they knew the *real* us. No one would love us if we stopped telling jokes and instead shared the heartbreaking truth that we feel like a big failure.

Loneliness is not reserved for those who are by themselves. Loneliness springs from wanting to be truly seen by another and not finding anyone to fill that role. This is why you can feel lonely even when you're married. When you feel as if your spouse doesn't understand you or perhaps your spouse has gotten so busy you feel unnoticed, you can feel very lonely.

Ultimately, our desire is actually to be one with Christ – to have a deep relationship with Him. When we do this, He is enough. We may still wish for other fulfilling relationships, but our worth comes Him, and we feel calm and stable in this love. Even when we know that Jesus should be the only relationship we need, it takes a great deal of maturity to let that be enough. I'm not sure I've ever rested completely in Jesus.

There are two major ways I know to combat the feeling of loneliness: Spending time with Jesus and serving others.

Spend Time With Jesus

Let all the earth keep silence before him.

- Let All mortal Flesh Keep Silence[xxiv]

This should hardly be surprising. If you're wallowing on your couch alone and you're not spending any time reading the Bible or a good Catholic book, that's a great place to start! Sometimes I'm not in the mood to read the Bible, and that's okay. There are tons of great fiction and non-fiction books written by faithful Catholics.

Since I have little kids, I can't always make it to the library. While that's pretty much a lazy excuse because I don't like driving, most libraries have a nice selection of eBooks now. You can check them out online, and you can read them on your Kindle. If you don't have a Kindle, you can download a free Kindle Reading App on your computer and read that way.

If you are blessed to have a perpetual Adoration chapel near you, go and spend time in Adoration. You don't have to go and pray silently on your knees the whole time. You can simply go and read a book or do some homework. I often like praying my rosary there. As long as you're respectful, do what makes you feel comfortable in Adoration.

Going to Adoration is a wonderful way to bask in the Lord's love. There's something so beautiful about being in His physical presence.

Volunteer For Others

Shepherds, why this jubilee?
Why your joyous strains prolong?
What the gladsome tidings be?
Which inspire your heavenly songs?

- *Angels We Have Heard on High*[xxv]

When I'm feeling down, and loneliness swirls around me like a dark cloud, the last thing I want to do is to go fake cheeriness in public. I'd rather wallow in a comfortable sweater with a warm cup of tea and stare into the endless pit of Netflix. I definitely favor denial and avoidance when it comes to dealing with black feelings.

But of course, this is no solution.

One of the best ways to get out of your funk is to go out and serve others. You won't *feel* like doing this, but it doesn't matter. You must get out of the house and go volunteer. During the holidays there are countless ways you can serve others. The more you focus on serving those in need, the more you'll let go of your bad attitude.

You'll start to see the many blessings God has given you. You'll begin to notice Jesus in the face of the people around you. It's an amazing gift to help people in need. When we pour ourselves into service, it really fills our own hearts in the end.

One year, I had two small kids, and I felt that there was no way I could volunteer. It's hard to serve soup with kids under five, and we didn't have a lot of money to go out and buy things for our parish wish list. I knew I needed some act of service to help me get my focus off of myself and onto others during the holiday season.

Eventually, we found a wonderful organization that housed the homeless for the winter months. They were always looking for volunteers to help stay overnight or man the shelter during the day. I knew I couldn't do either of those things, but I noticed they also needed food, specifically desserts. My girls and I were able to make some inexpensive brownies using a mix from Costco and simply drop them off.

It was a wonderful activity that I could share with my children. It warmed my heart knowing that these families who had no home might get some joy from a little dessert. They would be remembered. They would feel loved through this sugary treat that my family made.

If you try hard, you can find a way to serve others that works for your lifestyle and budget. The important thing is that you find someone in need and you do something nice for them. I find that this is one of the best ways to cure loneliness.

Who knows, you might even meet some friends in the process!

The Holidays Without Children

Away in a manger
No crib for a bed
The little Lord Jesus
Lay down his sweet head
The stars in the sky
Look down where he lay
The little Lord Jesus
Asleep on the hay

- *Away in a Manger*[xxvi]

One of the most painful aspects of celebrating the holidays can be the emptiness felt when there are no children in your home. This may be due to infertility, or perhaps your grown children have moved far away. This cross is particularly painful to bear since so many activities seem to be focused on kids. Every day, social media features pictures of children decorating gingerbread houses or sitting on Santa's lap.

This can feel like a constant reminder of your child-free home.

If you do not have any children of your own, I suggest you go out of your way to spend time with someone else's kids at Christmas. The holidays are magical when seen through children's eyes. It's why we enjoy being around them at Christmas time. Their wide eyes and big smiles take in the cheer of the holidays, and it warms our hearts to see their pure joy.

Maybe you have nieces or nephews. Maybe your college friends have started having children. You can always go to a nearby hospital and spend time with children who are stuck there for the holidays.

Instead of trying to bury your pain and avoid children, I believe seeking them out and serving them is the best way to help heal your broken heart. While nothing can fill the longing you have for a child, staying cooped up at home and wallowing in your empty nest will only lead to darkness and depression.

While it may still be painful to see children who are not your own enjoy the holidays, it will hurt less than sitting at home and listening to the lies that the devil will whisper into your ear.

Service and love are always weapons we can use to battle depression and evil.

Most people would be happy to let you participate in their fun children's activities and will probably be grateful for a helping hand! Keep praying to Jesus, Mary, and your favorite saints that they help you find peace with your situation. That doesn't mean you shouldn't keep asking for a child of your own, but ultimately we want to ask for the grace to accept God's will, whatever it is.

Depression

How silently, how silently
The wondrous gift is given!
So God imparts to human hearts
The blessings of His heaven.
No ear may hear His coming,
But in this world of sin,
Where meek souls will receive him still,
The dear Christ enters in.

- O Little Town of Bethlehem by Phillips Brooks[xxvii]

This is a heavy topic to talk about and one that I want to be careful with. Clinical depression should be handled by a medical professional. I will address clinical depression specifically in a following chapter. Because I'm not a doctor, I will not be giving any advice other than to share a few pointers for when I think you should go talk to a doctor about your depression.

What we're going to talk about in this section of the book are the feelings of sadness specifically brought about during the holidays. When we feel low, kind of blue, or sad about our situation, it's hard to remember that these feelings are temporary. We may feel them for many days in a row, but ultimately we have a choice. We can wallow in these feelings, or we can pick ourselves up and choose activities that lift us out of our depressive state.

I have a melancholic personality, so it's very easy for me to let one small incident spiral me down a dark path (e.g., needing to wrap presents but having no tape in the house).

I'll never be organized. I'm such a bad homemaker. I can't even do simple things like wrap a present. I'm such a terrible wife and friend.

I know that sounds extreme, especially over something as silly as not having tape, but that's how my mind works. I can choose to be a victim of this tendency or I can choose to recognize it, not give into those negative thoughts, and pick something positive instead.

The two ways I am proactive about battling depression and my running the negative thought track is to listen to positive affirmations and to flood my mind with scripture saturation!

Positive Affirmations (Prayer)

And then there did appear a Star,
Whose glory then did shine so far:
Unto the earth, it gave a great light,
And there it continued a day and a night.

- *The First Noel*[xxviii]

One of the most effective ways I've found for battling depression is through positive affirmations. I don't mean the "I attract wealth" kind of hokey/new age affirmations. I mean positive thoughts that help me saturate my brain with good, undeniably true thoughts instead of yucky ones.

Here are some examples of affirmations I say to myself throughout the day:

Sterling, you are loved.

You want to be a saint in Heaven.

God has endless mercy for you if you ask him.

You are a good wife.

You are a good mother.

You can do all things through Christ who strengthens you.

Be not afraid.

Offer up your suffering to God.

You can see that some of my affirmations are very simple and some are actually scripture verses. I have over 100 affirmations recorded in my own voice through an app called ThinkUp. It puts soft music in the background, and I can simply hit play on my phone and hear these affirmations play over and over again.

In addition to these affirmations, I also work on memorizing a verse with my children every week. This is something I learned to do when I was a Protestant. I learned to choose a verse for the week and to say that verse 100 times per day.

While that may seem like a difficult thing to do, it really isn't. I would carry a small piece of paper with me that had ten tabs ripped into one side. I would fold over a tab each time I said the verse ten times. It wouldn't be long when all ten tabs were folded over, and I had done my scripture memorization work for the day!

While there are many benefits to scripture memorization, the most powerful effect this practice has is that you are filling your brain with positive words, filling up your thought space, so there is no room for negative thoughts! If you're busy repeating scripture in your mind, you're not spending anytime putting yourself down or listing all things you wished you had this holiday season.

Because positive affirmations are often presented in a New Age/Attraction style, the entire practice is often thrown out. Positive affirmations can simply be a form of prayer that works for you. We live in a broken world where advertisements fill our minds with negative messages. We need to actively work to replace these lies with positive truths, especially ones rooted in scripture.

The first step into depression often involves our own negative voice and our poor self-image. If we can work on reprogramming our minds and rebuilding our self-esteem, we can stop the cycle that makes us feel depressed in the first place.

Red Flags Exercise

I find that most of us know which activities build us up and bring us genuine joy. We also know the activities that drag us down and make us feel worse about ourselves. We need to identify these bad activities and then surround them with RED FLAGS! When we feel drawn to participate in one of these activities, we need to instantly see that big red flag waving. This flag says, "Stop! This activity will cause you to feel depressed, and it will result in you wallowing in sadness. Don't do it!

Sit down and list the things you tend to do (or avoid doing) when you're feeling depressed. Here are some of my examples:

- I binge eat unhealthy food
- I spend hours watching television or reading books as a form of escapism
- I avoid my spouse or my children
- I stay at home and stop visiting with friends
- I stop taking showers or brushing my teeth

I have this list in my Catholic Mom Manifesto, which is a small booklet I keep with me to help me stay on track toward becoming a saint. I talk about why and how to create your own manifesto in my book *Catholic Mom Challenge*. I scan through this list often, and when I see that I'm doing one of these things, I know I need to snap out of it and choose activities that build me up instead.

The next step in the exercise is to make a list of activities that bring you out of a state of depression.

- Taking a meal to a mom who has just had a baby
- Taking a shower and putting on an outfit that makes me feel good
- Doing something fun and special with my children
- Going for a walk outside no matter what the weather is (even if only five minutes)

As with most problems, the first step to take when it comes to depression during the holidays is to acknowledge that this is indeed a problem you struggle with. The next step is to create strategies to help prevent this problem from happening. Get ahead of holiday depression this year by writing down triggers and signs that you're depressed. Then make a list of activities that bring you out of this mood.

If you really want to dig into some of your issues with depression, you can order *The Cognitive Behavioral Workbook for Depression* by William Knaus[xxix]. This is a step-by-step workbook that has you identify your triggers and come up with ways to avoid and overcome depression. It's an intense book but one I highly recommend if you really want to take control of your negative thought life and the patterns that lead you to and keep in depression.

Clinical Depression

Still, through the cloven skies, they come,
With peaceful wings unfurled,
And still their heavenly music floats
O'er *all the weary world;*
Above its sad and lowly plains,
They bend on hovering wing,
And ever o'er its babel sounds
The blessèd angels sing.

- It Came Upon A Midnight Clear by Edmund Sears[xxx]

Before we move on, I want to talk about clinical depression. I'm going to give you some difficult challenges this holiday season as well as tips to avoid anxiety and depression in the coming months. None of these will be effective, however, if you're suffering from clinical depression.

Dealing with sticky family situations, minimizing your decoration compulsion, reigning in gift giving… I know these are all tall orders. In no way am I suggesting that any of these are easy things to accomplish, but they are things you can work on if you're not clinically depressed.

The kind of depression I talk about overcoming in this book include things like negative self-talk, being in a bad mood, getting into a holiday funk, etc. I'm talking about staying in your pj's and watching Netflix and feeling bad the next day that you didn't get anything done. These are things that are part of a normal level of depression. When we have this kind of everyday depression, there are many ways we can snap ourselves out of this darkness and wallowing and move on.

You can go for a walk, take a shower, go to Adoration, or clean your kitchen. You may spend time in prayer and write down all the things you're grateful for and all the blessings Jesus has given to you. These are all ways to get you out of your funk and back on track.

Clinical depression, however, is different. It's a very real thing that you can't just pray your way out of or work yourself through by cleaning your home.

When you are clinically depressed, when you have an actual chemical imbalance in your body, you need professional help. I have suffered from clinical depression twice in my life. The first time lasted a few months after I graduated from college. The second time was postpartum depression after my second daughter was born.

Both times, I felt wretched about myself. That might be a stretch – most of the time I felt nothing, I felt dead inside. It was as if I knew things were important, but I couldn't get myself to care about them. I had lost my drive and my motivation to get anything done, even extremely important things.

I felt like I was covered in darkness. It was almost as if I was outside of my body looking at myself and thinking, "Sterling, why can't you just be your normal happy self?"

I wanted to be, but I couldn't seem to climb out of this dark fog. Both times, I met with a doctor and went on medication. Each time, I was able to go off of the medication after a few months. It was really amazing to me, both times, how quickly my body was able to stabilize. As soon as I would feel "like myself" again, I was able to more clearly see how depressed I really had been.

I'm not a doctor – but if you feel like you just can't get happy again and you can't connect with that person that you used to be, I would really encourage you to seek out professional help. Don't make a big deal out of it. Don't beat yourself up. Don't feel like a failure. Just go and talk with someone.

If you are clinically depressed, then it is not the time to take on really big challenges. Tuck this book away for later, because these tips will help you in the future, but now is not the time. Go see your family doctor or a psychologist and figure out what's going on. Try to find out if you have a chemical problem. You have to solve that before you try and solve any of the other problems we're talking about.

Anxiety

God rest you merry, Gentlemen,
Let nothing you dismay,
For Jesus Christ our Saviour
Was born upon this Day.
To save poor souls from Satan's power,
Which long time had gone astray.
Which brings tidings of comfort and joy.

- *God Rest You Merry, Gentlemen*[xxxi]

I say this in almost every talk I give. God did not design our bodies to live with anxiety. When we spend large amounts of time in an anxious state, it actually breaks down our bodies. We often experience physical symptoms as a result of our being too anxious. We get headaches, tummy aches, skin conditions, bathroom problems, and more just because we're flooding our system with too much cortisol (a steroid hormone released when stressed).

I find that my own anxiety stems from worrying too much. I worry about way too many things, especially things that aren't even real problems yet!

How many times have you gotten extremely anxious over something that may or may not happen in the future? Women are especially bad about doing this. We want everyone to be happy and safe. We are constantly worrying about things going the right way and keeping the peace. But all this worry is making us sick.

We lack sleep. We lack trust. We lack peace.

God does not want us to live this way. Jesus came so that we might have peace. He didn't come to make our lives easy, but He came to give us a promise. Repent and believe in the Gospels. That's it. His very simple message is the key to getting rid of anxiety.

Repent, which for us Catholics includes going to confession regularly after doing a thorough examination of conscience.

Believe in the Gospels. Read your bible, often. Really listen to what Jesus tells us. He tells us over and over again, "Be not afraid." The longer we go without reading these words, the harder it is for us to believe in them.

We must soak up God's word every single day. It's like an anchor that keeps us grounded in the storm. In the following chapter, I will share with you five tips for avoiding anxiety!

Five Tips For Avoiding Anxiety

I pray on Christmas
Oh, the sick will soon be strong
I pray on Christmas
The Lord will hear my song
I pray on Christmas
That God will lead the way
And I pray I really pray on Christmas
He'll get me through another day

- I Pray On Christmas by Harry Connick Jr.[xxxii]

Sometimes our life changes and we suddenly find ourselves feeling more anxious. This happened to me after my husband, and I bought a business and a few months in, it was sinking. I was working all the time, we were hemorrhaging money, I wasn't spending as much time with my kids, and I felt awful. Because I have read so much about anxiety, I suspected that a lot of my worries were really just fears about the future, not actual problems I was having in my current reality.

I bought the *Anxiety and Worry Workbook* by Dr. David Clark[xxxiii], and it really helped me to identify some of the fake things I was worried about and to deal with some of the real things I was anxious about. If you're a workbook kind of person, I highly recommend picking up a copy! I developed some strategies for avoiding anxiety.

Here are five tips I use for avoiding anxiety altogether:

1. **Breathe Deeply**

   Most of us breathe in a more shallow way that we should. When we take shallow breaths, our body things we are in danger. It thinks we are conserving energy to fight. Do it right now, start taking quick, shallow breaths. Notice, your brain starts looking around asking, "What's wrong?"

   The problem is that Americans now breath like this all the time! We do it without even realizing it! Our poor brain is looking around for the danger. It's keeping us in a heightened state of "let's get ready to battle!" This is causing our physical body a lot of problems.

   Instead, we must actively work on breathing deeply. Here's a good exercise to try and one I often do throughout the day: Breathe in to the count of six, hold your breath for two seconds and breathe out to the count of seven.

2. Be Grateful

   We already talked about how making a gratitude list can help combat loneliness. This works for anxiety too! The more we focus on the ways we are provided for by the Lord, the less we see what we don't have. We feel calmer when we see all the blessings around us.

We also feel that God genuinely loves us when we list out these blessings. We were designed to live in communion with God. When we feel as if our life is in ruins and that God has abandoned us, it is natural for us to feel anxious. It's like we're children who have been abandoned by our parents and we're left to fend for ourselves. Of course, we would feel anxious if this was true!

But it's not true. The Lord has not abandoned you. He is always with you. He loves you more than you can imagine and He has given you so many blessings. The more we focus on these blessings, the more we feel the love of the Father. The more we feel the love of the Father, the less anxious we become.

List things you're grateful for. Do this in a journal at night but also do this in your head all throughout the day. Think of all the blessings that God has given you.

3. **Go Outside**

We experience God in nature and in music. Most of us are pretty good at listening to music, but too many of us get so busy with our own lives that we forget to experience nature. We are holed up in our homes, our cars, our office buildings, and the many stores we have to go to, and we rarely stop to take in this beautiful world God created for us. Take a walk outside. Even if it's only for 3 minutes. Go outside and feel the fresh air on your face. Look around you. Notice the plants. Notice the sky. Smell the air. Even if you live in the city, you can see God's fingerprints everywhere.

You don't need to go on a two-hour hike to encounter God. Simply stepping outside and looking for Him right where you're at will help you find Him. And once you find Him, it will ease your anxiousness.

4. **Read Your Bible**

I know, I know, I'm a broken record about this, but it's because you're still not doing it! How do I know that? Because you're human and reading the Bible is often boring. Gasp! How can I say that? Because it's true.

There are many mornings I open it thinking, "Ugh, I don't want to read this boring book that is often confusing and fills me with guilt." But don't listen to those words. Those are the words of the devil. He has whispered them in my ear to keep me from seeing the doctor. I need the doctor to heal me from the wounds I receive in the world. I cannot be strong without the doctor.

You need the doctor too.

Don't put it off. Don't give into the warnings of the devil. Pull out your Bible. Read it every single day. Pour over the words of God and soak up His wisdom.

5. **Pray**

Sometimes we feel as if the anxiousness we experience is our own fault. If only we trusted in God more, we wouldn't feel anxious in the first place. And because we feel this sense of responsibility or guilt over our anxiety, we don't ask God to help us. But this is not what God wants at all.

He wants us to ask for help, every single time. He will never roll His eyes at you thinking, "Again? Really? Didn't we just deal with this?"

He will open up His arms, ask you to climb in His lap, give you the best hug you've ever received and say, "Tell me again, child."

Tell me again. And again.

He always wants to know about our pain. He is always there willing to show us mercy, to forgive us, and to pour out His love. All we have to do is show up and ask. Too few of us are humble enough to ask God for help over and over again.

It's as if we think we've hit some imaginary quota of prayer requests and now God is through with us.

Again, those are excuses the devil has planted in your ear. Take it to prayer. Take all your anxiety and your worry to the Lord. Ask God to remove your anxiety and to give you peace.

Just like depression, some people suffer from clinical anxiety and need professional help, maybe even medication. If you find that deep breathing, thinking about things you're grateful for, and going for a walk doesn't calm you down, go see a doctor to talk about what's going on.

When you feel yourself getting anxious, use these five tips above to try and calm down. If that doesn't work, talk with your spouse and consider seeing a professional for advice.

God did not design our bodies to handle anxiety and anger perpetually. The more we give in to these feelings, the more our physical bodies suffer.

Drink and Be Merry

When Joseph went to Bethlehem
I think he took great care
To place his tools and close his shop
and leave no shavings there.
He urged the donkey forward,
then, with Mary on its back,
And carried bread and goat cheese
in a little linen sack.

- *When Joseph Went to Bethlehem*[xxxiv]

For people who struggle with emotional eating like I do, the holidays can feel like a battlefield. Cookies, candies, and appetizers abound, and most of the time, they're free! Everyone is in a celebrating mood, and so the drinks are passed around and seconds are to be had.

While it can be easy to give in to this atmosphere and stuff your face with goodies and alcohol, the price can be high for those of us who just look at sliced cheese and gain four pounds. January rolls around, and we're left wondering, "Was it worth it?"

The answer for me is often no.

I want to encourage all of you this year to try something different. Instead of grazing on refined flour and sugar for two solid months, choose your party days wisely. My husband and I try to pick a few specific occasions when we partake of party food and drink, but we don't cheat any other time.

This strategy allows us to genuinely celebrate certain days with feasts, as is appropriate and encouraged in the Catholic Church, without giving way to gluttony and celebrating twenty-two days of feasting in the months of November and December.

Be strong.

Your health is not worth the few seconds it takes to scarf down cookies or spinach artichoke dip no matter how delicious they are. Give up the treats and instead, offer up your sacrifice to Christ for the conversion of souls this Christmas.

If you're trying to stay strong and limit the unhealthy food you eat, I highly suggest cutting out alcohol too. My resolve will be rock solid until I have half a glass of wine. Drinking alcohol affects the part of our brain that weighs risk-taking behavior it's common that after a few sips, you suddenly want to eat (or buy) something you had previously decided you didn't need.

Suddenly I forget that I want to be a healthy weight come January, and I dive into the desserts table with no remorse. I know this about myself, and so the first line in my defense against the delicious temptations is to abstain from alcohol. I know that one drink will make me lose my resolve and in the end, it's just not worth it for me.

If you know you're an emotional eater, set some rules for yourself before the temptations arise. You can download a free copy of A Catholic Guide to Overcome Emotional Eating on my website, and that will arm you with some ideas to stay strong this holiday season.

After all, God only gives us one body, and He asks that we take care of is a Holy temple!

Genuine Joy

Silent night, holy night,
Son of God, love's pure light;
radiant beams from thy holy face
with the dawn of redeeming grace,
Jesus, Lord, at thy birth,
Jesus, Lord, at thy birth.

- *Silent Night by Joseph Mohr*[xxxv]

I wanted to end this book with words about joy and evangelization. We often have this mixed up idea that joy is something that shows up all on its own. We think it's the warm, bubbly feelings we get when something wonderful happens!

Joy isn't like that at all.

Joy isn't a feeling; it's a choice. Just as we often hear that love is a choice, not a feeling, the same is true of joy, and yet this idea isn't talked about nearly as much. Joy is something we choose. The good news about that, like love, is that this is something we can cultivate to experience more of in our lives.

Feelings can be misleading. For example, someone can cause you physical pain by grabbing you too roughly. Just picture that for a moment, a man comes up behind you and grabs you so hard that it hurts your arms.

I feel awful just thinking about that.

What if I told you that you were chatting on your cell phone, about to walk into the street, and a large truck was about to hit you, but the man grabbed you just in time?

Now all of a sudden you are filled with great relief. You would probably feel an overwhelming sense of thankfulness to this man who stepped in and saved you!

The pain you experienced in your arm is a feeling you cannot control. It just happened. What you do control is your reaction to what happened. You can choose to be angry, or in this case, you can recognize that the pain was necessary and ultimately feel thankful that this stranger saved you from harm.

Joy is the reaction we have to the life we're living. We get to choose joy anytime we want!

You can easily look around and be grumpy at your lack of money, your dysfunctional family, or your constant state of singlehood. Alternatively, you can choose to smile – a really big smile – about the blessings God *has* given you.

If you are alive, breathing, and reading this right now, you are incredibly blessed. Just take a moment and let that sink in! The God of the Universe willed you into being, and you are alive right now. You have the time and freedom to be reading this book, even if you're paying the high price of toddlers destroying something in the other room! This freedom is pretty amazing.

I've often enjoyed this quote which is often attributed to Albert Einstein:

"There are only two ways to live your life. One is as though nothing is a miracle. The other is as though everything is."

One way we cultivate joy is by being the second type of person; choosing to see everything as a miracle! When it rains, be in awe of the rain. When the leaves turn colors, think of our amazing God who designed this world. The fact that you get to sleep in a warm, dry bed tonight is also a great gift that many people long for.

The key to having deep-down, unshakable and genuine joy is to be grateful for all these little things. One way to keep up this practice is to have a gratitude journal. It doesn't have to be fancy. You can staple some pieces of paper together.

The important part is that you start writing down all the things you're grateful for.

I'm grateful for this computer I'm working on and the electricity it's taking to run it. I'm grateful for the tea I'm drinking, and I know it's a luxury that I can afford tea. I'm grateful to hear my children laughing in their room enjoying their childhood and giving me this time to write.

It's easy to start listing things to be grateful for. And the wonderful part about gratitude is that the more you do it, the easier it becomes to do. It's like a big rolling snowball collecting joy along the way and growing so big that it fills your vision of the world with a lens of joy!

That is my wish for everyone this holiday season. That by believing in Jesus and seeing His wonderful works in the world, we may have genuine joy. I hope we will be filled with great awe and thankfulness that we are alive and that we will let this joy spill out onto the streets and into the hearts of everyone we meet.

Evangelization

Through each wonder of fair days God Himself expresses;
Beauty follows all His ways, as the world He blesses:
So, as He renews the earth, Artist without rival,
In His grace of glad new birth, we must seek revival.

- *Good King Wenceslas*[xxxvi]

As we near the time of the holidays, let us reflect on our role as Catholics in the world. It's easy for us to hide our light and feel nervous about sharing our faith. Few of us feel brave enough or perhaps prepared enough to share our faith with non-believers. But this is a lie that the devil whispers in our ears.

We do not need to be theologians to share our faith. Simply the way we live out our life is a great testament to our Catholic beliefs.

There are many small and subtle ways we can share our faith with the people we encounter. The easiest of all is to smile! A smile might seem like an insignificant thing, but to many lonely people, a smile is worth a great deal. We want to be Christ in the world, and that means bringing peace and joy wherever we go. Your attitude is a large billboard for Catholicism.

Imagine you were wearing a t-shirt that said, "Watch how a Catholic handles this situation?" Would you have been kinder yesterday? Would you have gone the extra mile to help people who were put in your path? Would you have spoken differently to your own family even?

Evangelization doesn't have to be a long sermon or hitting someone over the head with your Bible. You can evangelize with small phrases dropped into your everyday conversations.

"I have been so blessed recently…"

"I don't know what the future will bring, but I am trusting in God's will and His timing."

"I will ask God to give you peace in your situation."

"I've been praying that the Holy Spirit will guide me in my upcoming decision."

"I have been leaning on the Blessed Mother lately for support and encouragement."

These are small nuggets that you can drop into conversations. You don't have to try and convert everyone you meet with every conversation you have. You don't even have to explain yourself. You can drop in some Catholic language and move on. The seed will have been planted.

I know for my own extended family, my husband and I are the only Catholics. Whether they voice it or not, our family is looking to see how we act, how we speak, and how we treat others. We try our hardest to be Christ to them and to show what true forgiveness and mercy looks like.

We pray before entering their homes that the Holy Spirit guide our conversations so we can help lead them to Christ. We don't hide our Catholic faith, but we also don't use the holidays as a time to cram it down their throats either.

We want to exude an attitude of love and peace. We show that our hope is in the Lord and that we do no fear what is happening in the world around us.

People are attracted to peace and holiness. The more we can stay close to the Lord throughout the holidays, the more we will exude that peace and holiness. That is your mission this holiday season: draw close to the Lord and then spread that peace you receive everywhere you go! That is the heart of evangelization!

Be Intentional

O sisters too, how may we do
For to preserve this day
This poor youngling for whom we sing,
"Bye bye, lully, lullay"?

- Coventry Carol[xxxvii]

I believe in you. I'm confident that you can do the exercises in this book and have a better holiday season this year. It won't be perfect. You won't suddenly be able to overcome all the issues you've dealt with in the past, but you will feel like you have more control.

It has taken me years to get to the place where I actually look forward to the holidays. Don't expect that this happens overnight. If you keep working, though, it will happen!

The key to avoiding anxiety and depression during the holidays is to be intentional. Don't sleepwalk through your own life. Don't get stuck in avoidance and dread. Don't get so caught up in making other people happy that you end up with nothing but stress for yourself.

The holidays should be about love. At the end of the day, love is not a feeling; it's a choice. We love the people in our life by serving them. Be careful, though, there are positive and healthy ways to serve, and there are toxic ways to serve that actually end up hurting us.

Your job is to be intentional.

Be intentional about the tasks you take on and be intentional about finding peace in those tasks. It may be hard to go to Midnight Mass with your little children but, if you've committed to it, offer up your suffering for Christ and choose to have a good attitude. If it's not important to you that you go to Midnight Mass, and you're simply doing it out of peer pressure, either accept that you're doing it to feel more a part of the community or decline to go and attend Sunday morning if that's the kind of Christmas that would be better for your family!

This year is about trying on a new attitude and a new focus. You're going to be intentional about what you sign up for, you're going to be thoughtful when it comes to decorating and gift-giving, you're going to feel prepared to be with people you may not normally get along with, and you're going to do this all with Jesus and for Jesus.

Thanksgiving and Christmas are the perfect times to work on gratitude. This year I want you to focus on the great abundance of blessings that God has heaped onto your life.

Be Merry

Sing, choirs of angels, sing in exultation,
Sing, all ye citizens of Heaven above!
Glory to God, glory in the highest:
O come, let us adore Him, (3×)
Christ the Lord.

- Oh Come, All Ye Faithful by John Francis Wade[xxxviii]

Do you know what the holiday season is about? It's about Jesus Christ. The only son of God came down to Earth and became a man. That is utterly amazing! We've known this for over 2,000 years, and I think the shock and awe of it has faded.

Really think about it for a moment.

We get to go to Heaven because of Jesus. The lives we lead are full of selfishness and sinful behavior. We deserve to be far from God. We don't deserve to go to Heaven at all. God is fully justified in saying "Depart from me, you evildoers." We don't like to picture our God as angry and full of wrath, but He is. He does have righteous anger about each and every sin we commit.

Without Jesus, we would never get to be with God.

In His endless mercy, He sent Jesus to be our savior. In the quiet of the night, a baby was born in the small town of Bethlehem. This baby would be the King of Kings, and He would change the world.

This perfect, sinless man would grow up to be beaten, tortured, and killed for our sins. Even though we've probably sinned dozens of times by breakfast, we still have a shot at eternal salvation because of Jesus.

It's not just good news; it's incredible news!

It literally changed the world. We now live in a largely Christian world where people uphold Christian values. They may have been muddled throughout these last 2,000 years but trust me; the world is a much better place since Jesus came.

Christmas is about hope.

It's about the quiet anticipation of Jesus coming into the world and saving us in a way that we so desperately need, even now, 2,000 years later. And as we celebrate His birth, we are also looking to His second coming.

More than anything, we should be deeply grateful that we woke up this morning. You are alive! God chose you to be alive today. He has a unique job that only you can do. Your job is to pray and discern His will for your life and then do it.

It's not just Christmas that is about Jesus, although it really is a beautiful way for us to remember the quiet anticipation of our Lord's coming. Thanksgiving is also about Jesus because it is a time for us to give thanks to our maker for all our blessings. It is a time to help those who are less fortunate and to pray for those who have gone before us.

The holiday season is about joy, and all the world's genuine joy comes from the Lord. If you need to give yourself a pep talk every morning from November 1st to January 2nd to help you focus on the true meaning of the holidays – do it! It's not hokey at all.

What a wonderful act of the will.

Choosing to be kind and joyful even if you don't "feel" like it is one of the best gifts you can give to yourself and to everyone you interact with.

We talked about gifts: embracing minimalism and not going into debt. We talked about jealousy and squishing our envy bugs. We know that the more we focus on what other people have, the less we appreciate what we have. Jesus gave you, not only your blessings but your crosses as well. He gave you a perfect combination of life experiences to get you to Heaven...forever!

I don't know about you, but I don't want to sacrifice forever for some piddly little desire today.

The last thing we talked about is creating genuine joy this holiday season by focusing more on seeing people as souls. Realize that God has put every single person in our path to help find Heaven.

The best help we can offer is to let Christ shine through us, to show them unimaginable love and unimaginable forgiveness. That's what Jesus would do for every person he met on the street today.

This is difficult, and we're going to get this wrong, in some way, every single day. But it's our job to wake up the next morning and purpose to do better. We must be intentional about how we take care of the people in our lives and the resources which God has entrusted us.

We must strive for sainthood by being pure joy in the world, by treating others with real love. I wish you a very blessed holiday season and a very merry Christmas!

Acknowledgements

First, I have to thank God for sending his only son into the world knowing everything that would happen to Him. That God loved us so much that He would do this so we could have eternity in Heaven with Him is absolutely amazing to me!

I want to thank Cayla Mello for being the fastest editor ever! Thank you to everyone who gave me feedback and helped me choose the final cover design. Thank you to Lisa Ferry and Ashley Woleban for letting me pester you with questions about the holidays!

And lastly to all the Catholic women out there, you rock! You are beautiful, loved, and so needed. Don't for a minute let the world or the devil convince you that you're not enough. God thinks you're wonderful and I think you're wonderful.

Please go out into the world and be Jesus to everyone you meet. Shine His light and His love everywhere you go!

Can You Do Me A Favor?

Thank you for reading my book!

If you have any feedback or if you'd like to share how this book has affected you, please email me at letschat@sterlingjaquith.com.

If you could take a moment and leave me a review on Amazon, I would really appreciate it! New authors rely on reviews so readers will give them a chance.

Thank you again for being part of the Catholic Mom Challenge. I hope you enjoyed reading this book as much I enjoyed writing it!

About The Author

Sterling Jaquith lives in Boise, Idaho with her husband and their four children. She has a degree in finance from Seattle University and is a certified dog trainer. She blogs at www.sterlingjaquith.com and her podcast *Coffee & Pearls* comes out on Tuesdays.

Her husband Michael Jaquith has a podcast, *The Catholic Commute*, that comes out on Mondays and Wednesdays designed for men to listen to on their way to work! You can read more about his projects at www.thestakesarehigh.com.

Sterling loves speaking at conferences and retreats, sharing her conversion story and the message that we should all be striving for sainthood! You can read more of her writings at www.Catholic365.com and www.catholicmom.com.

Catholic Mom Challenge

Read another book by Sterling, Catholic Mom Challenge available at Amazon in Kindle and paperback format!

Filled with practical exercises and worksheets, this book is about helping moms figure out how to strive for sainthood among the piles of laundry, the mounting to-do list, and the stress of getting dinner ready!

The Catholic Mom Challenge system blends the power of Catholicism with discrete steps that busy moms can take to manage their lives while still striving for sainthood. This system works for everyone because it will teach you to always be refining what works for you.

Not Of This World

Read another book by Sterling, Not of This World available at Amazon in Kindle and paperback format!

All Catholics are called to practice minimalism. How do we navigate our modern society without giving into consumerism and materialism? How do you practice minimalism with a large family? What does homeschooling minimalism look like? What if you have roommates or a multi-generational household? Do we have to give up our smartphones?

Follow Sterling on a journey as she explains how minimalism will bring you more peace and freedom. She will guide you step-by-step through your home with suggestions for how to embrace this lifestyle all at once or in baby steps.
And yes, you can keep your smartphone!

End Notes

[i] https://en.wikipedia.org/wiki/Angels_from_the_Realms_of_Glory
[ii] https://en.wikipedia.org/wiki/Hark!_The_Herald_Angels_Sing
[iii] https://en.wikipedia.org/wiki/What_Child_Is_This%3F#Lyrics
[iv] https://www.songandpraise.org/a-christmas-carol-christmas-hymn.htm
[v] "16 Personalities," 12 Sept. 2016 <http://www.16personalities.com>.
[vi] Katie Warner, Head and Heart: Becoming Spiritual Leaders for Your Family (Emmaus Road Publishing, 2015).
[vii] https://en.wikipedia.org/wiki/O_Holy_Night
[viii] https://en.wikipedia.org/wiki/O_come,_O_come,_Emmanuel
[ix] https://www.catholicdoors.com/songs/xmas/song114.htm
[x] https://en.wikipedia.org/wiki/I_Saw_Three_Ships
[xi] https://en.wikipedia.org/wiki/Home_for_Christmas_(Amy_Grant_album)
[xii] Fr. Michael Gaitley, 33 Days To Morning Glory (Marian Press, 2011).
[xiii] Saint Louis de Montfort, True Devotion (Monfort Pubns, 1984).
[xiv] https://en.wikipedia.org/wiki/Go_Tell_It_on_the_Mountain_(song)
[xv] https://en.wikipedia.org/wiki/Do_You_Hear_What_I_Hear%3F
[xvi] https://en.wikipedia.org/wiki/I_Wonder_as_I_Wander
[xvii] Elizabeth Scalia, Little Sins Mean A Lot (Our Sunday Visitor, 2016)
[xviii] https://en.wikipedia.org/wiki/We_Three_Kings
[xix] https://en.wikipedia.org/wiki/In_the_Bleak_Midwinter
[xx] "We Choose Virtues," 7 Nov. 2016 <https://www.wechoosevirtues.com/>.
[xxi] https://en.wikipedia.org/wiki/Here_We_Come_A-wassailing
[xxii] https://en.wikipedia.org/wiki/O_Holy_Night
[xxiii] http://catholicdoors.com/songs/xmas/song012.htm
[xxiv] https://en.wikipedia.org/wiki/Let_all_mortal_flesh_keep_silence
[xxv] https://en.wikipedia.org/wiki/Angels_We_Have_Heard_on_High
[xxvi] https://en.wikipedia.org/wiki/Away_in_a_Manger
[xxvii] https://en.wikipedia.org/wiki/O_Little_Town_of_Bethlehem
[xxviii] https://en.wikipedia.org/wiki/The_First_Noel
[xxix] The Cognitive Behavioral Workbook for Depression by William Knaus
[xxx] https://en.wikipedia.org/wiki/It_Came_Upon_the_Midnight_Clear
[xxxi] https://en.wikipedia.org/wiki/God_Rest_You_Merry,_Gentlemen
[xxxii] https://en.wikipedia.org/wiki/I_Pray_on_Christmas
[xxxiii] Anxiety and Worry Workbook by Dr. David Clark
[xxxiv] http://ldsguy.tripod.com/Christmas.carols.html
[xxxv] https://en.wikipedia.org/wiki/Silent_Night
[xxxvi] https://en.wikipedia.org/wiki/Good_King_Wenceslas
[xxxvii] https://en.wikipedia.org/wiki/Coventry_Carol
[xxxviii] https://en.wikipedia.org/wiki/O_Come,_All_Ye_Faithful

49875914R00077

Made in the USA
Middletown, DE
24 October 2017